THE THREE GRACES OF VAL-KILL

The Three Graces of Val-Kill

ELEANOR ROOSEVELT,

MARION DICKERMAN, AND

NANCY COOK IN THE PLACE

THEY MADE THEIR OWN

Emily Herring Wilson

THE UNIVERSITY OF

NORTH CAROLINA PRESS

Chapel Hill

This book was published with the assistance of the William R. Kenan Jr. Fund
of the University of North Carolina Press.

The University of North Carolina Press has been
a member of the Green Press Initiative since 2003.

Front cover: Stone Cottage at Val-Kill and Nan Cook, Marion Dickerman,
and Eleanor Roosevelt; back cover: monogrammed linen from Stone Cottage.
Courtesy of the Cook-Dickerman Collection, Eleanor Roosevelt National
Historic Site, National Park Service

Library of Congress Cataloging-in-Publication Data
Names: Wilson, Emily Herring, author.
Title: The three Graces of Val-Kill : Eleanor Roosevelt, Marion Dickerman,
and Nancy Cook in the place they made their own / Emily Herring Wilson.
Description: Chapel Hill : The University of North Carolina Press, [2017] |
Includes bibliographical references and index.
Identifiers: LCCN 2017015854| ISBN 9781469635835 (cloth : alk. paper) |
ISBN 9781469635842 (ebook)
Subjects: LCSH: Roosevelt, Eleanor, 1884–1962. | Dickerman, Marion, 1890–
1983. | Cook, Nancy, 1884–1962. | Female friendship—New York (State)—
Hyde Park (Dutchess County) | Feminism—New York (State) | Eleanor
Roosevelt National Historic Site (N.Y.) | Val-Kill Industries.
Classification: LCC E807.1.R48 W473 2017 | DDC 305.4209747—dc23
LC record available at https://lccn.loc.gov/2017015854

FOR ED

"Till time and times are done"

CONTENTS

A section of photographs begins on page 87

THE THREE GRACES OF VAL-KILL

PROLOGUE

Dear Hyde Park. —Sara Delano Roosevelt

Let us imagine the Hudson Valley in late summer of 1924, in the Roosevelt house called Springwood at Hyde Park, on a day that began like any other day: fires were lit, kitchen pots were heated, heavy drapes were pulled back, and sunlight fell upon old carpets. Overhead the sounds of running feet broke open the silence. Sara Delano Roosevelt, sole mistress of the house since "Mr. James" had died almost twenty-five years ago, had been awake and listening, and she opened her arms to receive the grandchildren in her bed. Then she dressed, calling to her son Franklin to remind him that breakfast would be served downstairs. When she passed her daughter-in-law Eleanor's door she knocked lightly, listened, and moved on. From the stairs to the lower floor she could smell the acrid smoke left by Franklin's friends, who had stayed late. She sniffed—not her husband's fine cheroot—and moved into her snuggery to greet the servants and ready herself for the day's inspections of the barns and fields, a task she had once shared with James. After all these years without him she could still feel his presence in the house. The great front door swung open, revealing a flash of fall color in the trees. Along the Albany Post Road wagons moved, and the village was already stirring. To the west, below the bluff, the Hudson River was its own master. A lone boatman floated downstream.

When Eleanor slipped into an empty place at the breakfast table between Marion Dickerman and Nancy Cook, life partners, Eleanor's closest friends, and her invited guests for the weekend, Sara nodded. Breakfast was served from the sideboard, with Franklin's favorite, kedgeree. From his end of the table Franklin smiled and began joking with his sons. Daughter Anna looked at her mother and said nothing.

Something seemed different; family tensions had eased. Marion and Nan understood that Eleanor was happier after Franklin's suggestion yesterday that the three women build a weekend cottage for themselves on land he would lease them on the banks of Fall-Kill Creek in the part of the Hyde Park estate called Val-Kill. What lay ahead was unclear. Franklin was still recovering from the effects of polio, and his political future was still out of sight, but he and his selfless friend and closest adviser, Louis Howe, held out hope, however uncertain it seemed at this time, that he might one day achieve his dream—to be president of the United States. Eleanor's future was less clear in her mind, but she knew that her unhappy marriage, life under the dominance of her mother-in-law, and the prospect of the last of her five children leaving home for boarding school made it necessary for her to make changes, too. What enabled her to take the next steps were these two friends, the independence she would gain from living at Val-Kill, and a wider progressive network of other women. Eleanor did not like to be alone, and many of the happiest times of her life were those when she worked with groups sharing the same public interests. The women she met in Democratic politics in New York in the early 1920s showed her the way.

Historians have recognized Eleanor Roosevelt as the most influential First Lady in American public life, advocating for justice for all, but she sought to define her legacy for herself in a different way when she said, "I think perhaps I would prefer when I am dead to have it said that I had a gift for friendship."[1] This is the story of one friendship—with Marion and Nan—and Eleanor's first bold experiment, creating a female-centered household that was liberating in its new possibilities for an independent life.

The Three Graces of Val-Kill is a work of evocation and reflection, based on historic research, interviews, and travel. My purpose is to find new ways to better understand one of the most written about women in American history before she became known as the great Eleanor Roosevelt. One of the neglected chapters in her biography is the decade in which she established her independence before becoming First Lady. This critical period was marked by her friendship with Marion Dickerman and Nancy Cook. The women FDR called the "Three Graces" created a community in Hyde Park that supported their personal growth, their career interests, and FDR's own political needs.

Although over several years I have extensively read Roosevelt studies and primary documents at the Franklin D. Roosevelt Library and Museum in Hyde Park, my inspirational sources for this book have been my visits to Val-Kill, to the Roosevelt summer home on Campobello Island, and to the historic New Deal housing project at Arthurdale, West Virginia, called "Eleanor's Little Village." Wherever I have gone, woodland walks have given me time to think about my research in the archives, and guides and fellow visitors have encouraged my questions. In writing this book, I have been carefully true to the "facts": when I describe scenes, they are accurate representations of times and places, and all quotations from individuals come directly from either primary or secondary sources. This story illuminates what we can see and understand; at the same time I recognize that we cannot see everything that happened out of our sight so long ago. I am reminded of the poet A. R. Ammons's question in "Unsaid": "Have you listened for the things I have left out?" I respect Eleanor Roosevelt's wise constraint: "It seems as though one can find privacy only within the silence of one's own mind."[2] Readers who reflect upon these matters themselves will, I hope, find their own way to a deeper understanding of Eleanor Roosevelt and of friendship and family: Eleanor Roosevelt belongs to the ages. The journey to Val-Kill begins.

1

THE HUDSON RIVER VALLEY

I guess it is bred in me to love it. — Eleanor Roosevelt

The Roosevelts and the Hudson River Valley are intimately linked in every telling of their story, and to appreciate how much Franklin and Eleanor loved it we should visualize the setting that dominates this book. Then we can understand how that love of place provided essential comfort and solace in some of the best and worst of times for each of them. For Eleanor and her friends, a hidden corner of the Hyde Park estate gave them a home of their own at the same time it kept them close to FDR's ambitions to become president of the United States. The place was essential to everything that Eleanor and Franklin became.

The Hudson River Valley, like human nature, both endures and changes over time. A sense of place endures, for what the seventeenth-century Dutch settlers saw we can still see today—the broad river, sometimes ruffled by whitecaps; the high bluffs; gray skies, blue skies; the distant Catskills; and the interior creeks and marshes— all made more dramatic by a sudden flash of lightning in a summer storm, a sweep of cold wind, colors of spring and fall, sunrise, and moonlight. If we look back in time, we may also see a man on horseback, a family in a sleigh, a team of cutters hauling blocks to icehouses, a steamboat carrying goods to the city, a farmer in a field, a shopkeeper in a village, or, bending toward our story, a woman whose long stride carries her away from a manor house high above the river into deeper woods and a cottage with a fire burning in the grate. We have arrived at the setting for our story.

The town of Hyde Park, established by state law in 1821, encompasses land whose ownership dates back to the late 1600s, when Dutch businessmen granted deeds by the English Crown purchased several thousand acres from the Wappinger Indians. The seventeenth-century farming community of wheat fields and meadows occupying flatlands set back from the river evolved into rural estates sustained by city money earned in banking and investments. In the 1800s Hyde Park became the site of country homes for some forty or so "river families," many of them seasonal residents. The confluence produced two strains of American history: villages of small farmers and shopkeepers (life as it was lived) and landed estates of wealthy aristocrats (life as it should be lived, according to Sara Delano Roosevelt). Locals distinguished the two groups as "the Village" and "the River," and of course they did not meet on equal ground: when farming failed, local families went to work in the big houses. At the Dutchess County Fair, established in 1842, both groups were neighborly, and if the rich man won ribbons for his stables, local cooks took prizes for their kitchens. At Christmas the squire and his lady distributed turkeys for their employees on The Place, as Sara Delano Roosevelt fondly called Springwood. And when a child was sick in the village, there was help at hand from Mrs. Roosevelt, who believed in noblesse oblige, telling her son, "One can be as democratic as one likes, but if we love our own, and if we love our neighbors, we owe a great example."[1]

Hyde Park in those days was thus a place of great houses and small farms. When the farms failed, the essential character of Hyde Park remained: a rural landscape of villages where the library, founded by Sara Delano Roosevelt, served a community of farmers, school teachers, and estate owners. (Mrs. Roosevelt and Mrs. Frederick Vanderbilt donated large numbers of books.)

Hyde Park was among the earliest of the villages the Dutch settled along the eastern bank of the 150-mile-long Hudson River, equidistant from the state capital at Albany and New York City. The village itself was small, limited by the river to the west and by the vast estates of wealthy families to the east. In the mid-nineteenth century, the American artists of the Hudson River School made the picturesque landscape famous with their large paintings of clouds, mountains, bluffs, waterfalls, rivers, and verdant banks. The paintings only hinted at the threats pastoral America was facing from the industrialists who dominated the commercial landscape.

During the Gilded Age some forty or fifty of America's wealthiest northeastern businessmen built mansions on the bluffs with dramatic views of the river. In seasonal migrations, women, children, tutors, nurses, baggage, and barrels packed with china and silver moved back and forth. Some came on the steamboat *Mary Powell* and were delivered to the wharf in Poughkeepsie. Others traveled by train from fashionable brownstones and palatial houses in New York City to the rural hinterlands of Dutchess County. The train station at Hyde Park was lively with arriving families met by their carriages and drivers to transport them to the big houses made ready by housekeepers, maids, cooks, butlers, gardeners, and groomsmen. Fires were lit in marble fireplaces to throw off the chill of a house that had been closed up, waiting for the owners' return.

Two neighboring families at Hyde Park, more friendly acquaintances than close friends, became among the best-known names in American history—the Vanderbilts for making money, and the Roosevelts for making history. The Vanderbilts were new money and built more and showier houses, the one at Hyde Park a fifty-four-room Beaux Arts mansion with Italianate gardens. The 1795 farmhouse Squire James Roosevelt purchased in 1867 had only seventeen rooms and was modest by comparison, but the location was splendid—a high bluff at Crumb Elbow, a bend on the Hudson River.

James Roosevelt could afford to present himself more modestly: his ancestry dated back to the Dutch settlers of Old Amsterdam, and he was a member of New York's Knickerbocker society. He and his first wife, Rebecca, bought the clapboard house with 110 acres—which included a horse-trotting track, stables, and a rose garden behind a high hedge—as a country retreat. Almost immediately he began adding land to his estate, which when he died amounted to 700 acres. He also added more rooms and indoor plumbing to the old house and named it Springwood. James and Rebecca and their son, James Roosevelt ("Rosy," who was to marry an Astor and live nearby), traveled by private railcar from their elegant townhouse on Washington Square in New York City to spend spring and fall at Hyde Park. In summers they traveled around Europe and to Campobello Island in New Brunswick, Canada.

After Rebecca died, James, now fifty-two, married the attractive Sara Delano, a spinster at twenty-six, who lived across the river on her family's estate, Algonac. Sara was pregnant when they returned to Springwood from their long European honeymoon, and she gave birth to their first and only child, Franklin, in the upstairs bedroom. When he was four years old, Franklin met his fifth cousin on the Oyster Bay side of the Roosevelt family, Eleanor, age two, when she was brought to Hyde Park to visit her "Aunt Sally."

Sara inherited all of the estate when James died in 1900, and she had no intention of giving up control. She called Franklin home from Harvard to share her grief and travel with her to Europe. When Franklin went back to his studies, his mother took a house in Boston to be near him. They formed a twosome that lasted until Sara died in 1941, almost four years before Franklin. Springwood belonged to Sara, and Franklin, even as an adult, struggled to maintain his independence. Biographers have suggested that her possessiveness led to his lifelong habit of concealing his private feelings. Certainly he became a master at deception.

In the summer of 1902 on the train from New York City to Tivoli, her Grandmother Hall's home on the Hudson, Eleanor, age eighteen, had her first serious talk with her cousin Franklin, age twenty, who was returning with his mother to Hyde Park. He and Eleanor had a long conversation, and he was so taken with her intelligence that he walked her to the next car to see his mother. When he fell in love with Eleanor, he kept it secret from Mama as long as he could, and then agreed to her wish to keep the engagement secret for another year.

Marrying young is a way to assert independence, and perhaps that is one reason why Franklin at twenty-one and Eleanor at nineteen fell so quickly in love. It was also to his advantage, as an only child, to have someone between him and his mother. Sara, for her part, tried to be generous and kind: she invited Eleanor to the family summer home at Campobello, where Eleanor and Franklin managed to keep out of her sight with long walks on the island. Sara met Eleanor in the city for shopping and for tea and invited her to house parties at Springwood. When Franklin attempted to keep his mother from knowing how often he was seeing Eleanor, Eleanor urged him to tell her the truth. Orphaned as a child of ten by the deaths of both parents (she was eight when her mother died from diphtheria; almost two years later her father died from alcoholism), Eleanor had even more reason to want a home of her own after years of living with relatives. She was grateful at last to have found a loving home with a stable mother figure, although almost immediately Sara Delano Roosevelt would prove to be a daunting mother-in-law.

Sara might have wanted Franklin and Eleanor to marry at Hyde Park, but getting married in New York City conferred an advantage the politically ambitious Franklin could not resist: on 17 March 1905, Eleanor's Uncle Theodore, newly elected president of the United States, could combine his attendance at the city's St. Patrick's Day parade with giving away his niece in marriage at the twin houses of her Aunt Susie and Susie's mother, Mrs. Ludlow. After the wedding, Sara remained in the city while Franklin and Eleanor went to Springwood for a ten-day honeymoon, alone except for Elspeth McEachern, Sara's faithful and observant Scottish housekeeper. Eleanor suspected that Elespie thought she was not good enough for Master Franklin.

When Anna was born to Eleanor and Franklin in 1906, Sara was delighted and immediately took charge of her—as she did of the children who followed. Four of Eleanor and Franklin's six children (a son died in infancy) were born in New York houses outfitted by Mama, and all were brought to Hyde Park for family occasions.

Sara and Franklin made significant additions to Springwood, both to accommodate his large family and to create a more imposing residence for a man with presidential aspirations, and by 1915 the house had thirty-five rooms. The third floor was for the children, with bedrooms and a nursery as well as a playroom and separate bedrooms for the nurse and governess. The estate bore the imprint of Sara and Franklin—her snuggery, his library; her music room, his study; her farm (with homegrown foods for the table), Franklin's fields and trees. Eleanor later complained that she had no say-so in the household, was not allowed in the kitchen, and learned nothing about how to manage a house and a family. At first, however, she was compliant and grateful, and unwilling to confront Mama or Franklin.

In New York City, Sara Delano Roosevelt built twin townhouses— one for Franklin and his family at 49 East 65th Street, and one for her next door at number 47 (not an unusual arrangement for wealthy Manhattan families). Interior doors on three floors allowed Sara to appear whenever and wherever she chose. At Hyde Park, Eleanor, Franklin, and the children lived under one roof in Sara's house. Wherever they lived, Eleanor (and Franklin) understood that Sara believed that a house should be run for the man. And she believed that Eleanor and Franklin's children belonged to her. All their lives, when they wanted something, they would look toward their grandmother, who claimed that she was their real mother—and indeed, they often spent more time with Sara than with their own mother and father. And the children, like Franklin, thought of Hyde Park as home. Eleanor felt like a visitor.

•

Eleanor and Franklin had been deeply in love when they honeymooned at Springwood, but in 1918 her discovery of Franklin's affair with Lucy Mercer, her young social secretary, changed her feelings (apparently Eleanor destroyed Franklin's courtship letters to her after the discovery). Eleanor had read Lucy's love letters to Franklin when she unpacked his suitcases after he returned from his U.S. military operations overseas during World War I, confirming her worst suspicions about her husband's frequent absences from her over the past year. The affair had taken place in Washington, D.C., when Franklin was assistant secretary of the navy and Eleanor and the children were at the Roosevelts' house on Campobello Island. The fact that Alice Roosevelt Longworth, Theodore's daughter and Eleanor's cousin, encouraged the somewhat clandestine relationship and that others knew about it as well in the gossipy circles of Washington deepened the humiliation. Eleanor was devastated, but the marriage would endure. Sara may have cast the determining vote on that by threatening to cut Franklin out of her estate if he left Eleanor. Franklin wanted to get past the crisis as quickly and as silently as possible, and Springwood, even with a rowdy family of young children, was big enough for a man and his wife to maintain some distance from each other.

In 1921 an even more dramatic turn of events changed the Roosevelts' lives yet again: Franklin was stricken by polio in the summer home on Campobello Island, and everything, included Springwood, had to be modified to suit the needs of a man in a wheelchair. Eleanor moved out of the second-floor bedroom that she and Franklin had shared and into a small bedroom between his and Mama's. Eleanor could explain in the months immediately following the change that Franklin needed physical therapists and valets to be in and out of his room at all hours, but she never returned.

How the move to another bedroom reflected Eleanor's needs is less clear. Her adult children believed that she no longer wanted to sleep with their father, but children's knowledge of their parents' sex life is speculative. What is clear is that she changed the way she lived at Springwood. Leaving altogether was never an option. The Hudson River Valley was Eleanor's to love as much as it was Franklin's and Sara's. She traveled the world, but she always came back to the valley. She did not want to live far from home.

•

Eleanor's roots in the Hudson River Valley were as deep as Franklin's. Like Sara Roosevelt, Eleanor's maternal Grandmother Hall had a New York City house and migrated from the city to her 1872 estate, Oak Terrace, north of the river town of Tivoli, twenty miles up the Albany Post Road from Hyde Park. In 1892, after her daughter Anna's death, Grandmother Hall took in Eleanor—whom they called "Totty"—and her younger brother, Hall. "There are sad memories as well as happy ones," Eleanor later said of those years, "but I shall never know any place, or any house as well as I know that one."[2] The house at Tivoli was a mansion with many rooms and servants, but unlike Franklin's home at Hyde Park, it was a dark place. Grandmother Hall prayed a great deal in a household made unruly, and sometimes dangerous, by the reckless behavior of her alcoholic sons. Grandmother Hall passed along her strict puritanical views and strong sense of duty to her granddaughter.

Eleanor's mother and aunts were attractive women of great personality, and her Hall relations believed that Eleanor had inherited from them her own particular family charm. As a young child she found her pleasures outside the decaying house—rising with Aunt Pussie before breakfast to row five miles down the river to pick up the mail and in the afternoons lying on the grass under a tree reading a book. Her summers at Tivoli fed Eleanor's need for romance, especially after her father's death from bouts of drinking and depression, when she needed to fantasize the father she called the love of her life. She could recall steamboat whistles, playing tennis, sledding, and horseback riding, and, when her grandmother allowed it, sometimes visiting her relations at Oyster Bay (the Theodore Roosevelt side of the family) and in mansions up and down the river. She loved the sounds of birds in the trees and frogs in the marshes; she loved weather and seasons, especially fall in the Hudson Valley; and she loved long walks. To the end of her life she would return to Tivoli, visiting relatives (her mother's sister, her Aunt Maude, after marrying David Grey, returned to live some years at the old home place), taking her grandchildren to walk through the abandoned halls—able to feel beauty others could not see in the empty house.

•

About two miles through the woods from Springwood there is a place called Val-Kill, named for Fall-Kill Creek (Dutch for "valley stream"). Fall-Kill is an active stream, racing or meandering according to the weather. Val-Kill included the large Bennett farm, which Franklin purchased in 1911 and rented to tenants. The land on the other side of the rough bridge crossing the creek elevates slightly uphill to a plateau. After Franklin was crippled by polio, the hillside became a favorite picnic place where he could get away from the Big House for diversion and privacy, and he had rough roads cleared so that he could drive there in his car equipped with hand controls.[3] Eleanor and the children often joined him for picnics on the hillside, and after a while Eleanor began to invite her two closest friends, Marion Dickerman and Nancy Cook, whom Franklin liked. He did not mind if they saw his shrunken legs as he stretched out on a blanket. They were like family. Val-Kill would be the place where Eleanor, Marion, and Nan built a cottage for themselves.

The Roosevelts lived differently from the local citizens, of course, but they were not like the family portrayed in Thomas Cole's famous 1846 painting *The Picnic*, which shows ladies in long dresses and gentlemen in coats and straw boaters lounging or pouring wine, wicker baskets filled with food, a troubadour, and well-behaved children sitting quietly around their own picnic cloth near a clear lake with a boat and the Catskills in the background. Val-Kill bore little resemblance to the paintings of the Hudson Valley School; in fact, it could have been anywhere on a farm where there was a rickety bridge, a creek with thick marsh grasses at water's edge, and a scattering of scrub trees and thickets.

Nature manifested at Val-Kill in what Eleanor called the "drama of life" — a great blue heron, frogs calling, cedar trees and vines, meadows, and ragged roads and trails. The setting was ideal — private but not remote. And there were good neighbors — not Vanderbilts and Astors but Johannesens and Smiths, men and women who did their own work and shared their vegetables and preserves. The distance in spirit between Val-Kill and Springwood was greater than the actual two miles, and some friends coveted Eleanor's invitation to a Val-Kill picnic more than an invitation to the Big House.

Near Springwood there is another special Roosevelt place: on Route 9, the old Albany Post Road, St. James Episcopal Church was Sunday home to the Roosevelts and other river families, as well as the families who worked for them. The church was founded in the early 1800s by congregants from Christ Episcopal Church in Poughkeepsie. James Roosevelt was senior warden most of his life. Sara, a Unitarian, had become an Episcopalian when she married James, and together they attended services, held in the chapel in the village in cold weather because there was no heat in the small church. Franklin had been baptized and confirmed at St. James and in 1907 was elected senior warden, to serve for the rest of his life. A stained glass window at St. James honors the memory of his father.

Eleanor, a lifelong Episcopalian confirmed at the Church of the Incarnation in New York City, likewise attended services at St. James when she was at Hyde Park. She especially loved Christmas Eve, when she gathered up the houseguests and took them with her. Franklin and the children often had to be coaxed into going. Eleanor believed that the church had a place in an individual's life, a belief sustained more by the ritual than by theology, and she cherished the intimacy and spirituality of the little church. Local housewives and shopkeepers and river families knelt together, though for a long time the river families maintained separate pews with nameplates on the entries. The Roosevelts occupied the third-row pew on the left, but if a visitor or member happened to be sitting there, Eleanor simply found another seat. The church continued to maintain the Roosevelt pew long after the old pew customs had lapsed. Eleanor faithfully paid her yearly church pledge, put several dollar bills in the collection plate at each service, and sang the hymns she had sung in Grandmother Hall's home on Sunday nights. The rector knew her well, as did the other parishioners, and after church she sometimes spontaneously invited those who were alone to Val-Kill for lunch. Among the local members was Henrietta Nesbitt, a celebrated baker. Eleanor would order Henrietta's famous doughnuts to be sent to Albany when Franklin was governor and later brought her to the White House as the housekeeper.

The Book of Common Prayer contained the language and the services Eleanor had heard all her life. When the priest welcomed all to partake of the Holy Communion, intoning, "Lift up your hearts," Eleanor and other worshippers responded, "We lift them up unto the Lord," and met at the marble altar.

Outside and a few steps away from the church is the graveyard where James and Rebecca, and later Sara, were buried side by side. Nearby is a small stone marking the burial place of Eleanor and Franklin's fourth child, the first Franklin Jr. She never forgot the burial of her infant child and her horror at leaving him in the cold ground. If for no other reason than that, she could never move away from Hyde Park.

Nearby Poughkeepsie, the Dutchess County seat, was an agricultural market town where locals gathered to shop. As a child riding the train with her grandmother, Eleanor loved the Poughkeepsie station, where a black man got on and peddled wares from a nearby café. The railroad station was on the west side of town with a view of the river and the industrial properties that lined its banks. Much of Poughkeepsie's history is tied to the river, home to eighteenth-century sloops and nineteenth-century steamboats carrying passengers and commerce. Vassar College, two miles from the town, was founded in 1865 by Matthew Vassar, Poughkeepsie's leading citizen. In later years Eleanor would meet students there and make close friends among the faculty women, many of whom shared homes off campus where good food and lively conversations reminded her of her beloved teacher, Mlle. Marie Souvestre, and her adolescent school days at Allenswood, a boarding school for girls in London. Vassar would give her some of the college experience she had never had.

History had drawn the Roosevelt narrative map, and Eleanor would make her own place on it.

2

NEW YORK CITY AND THE NEW WOMAN

Miss Cook and Miss Dickerman and I had become friends in just the way that
Miss Lape and Miss Read and I had been first drawn together through the work
we were doing. This is one of the most satisfactory ways of making and keeping
friends. — Eleanor Roosevelt

When Mrs. Franklin D. Roosevelt entered the crowded hotel ballroom
in New York City in June 1922, many of the one hundred women present turned to look. Everybody recognized her from the newspaper
accounts of her travels with Franklin when he had campaigned as
James Cox's vice president on the unsuccessful 1920 national Democratic ticket, and those who knew her watched the surprise register
on the faces of those who were seeing her in person for the first time.
She was so much more youthful than she seemed in her photos. Some
wondered if her fur wrap had belonged to her mother-in-law, who
was already seated near the front (it had). Although Eleanor was nervous about being the keynote speaker for the New York Democratic
Women's fund-raiser, she radiated a magnetic warmth that energized
the room.[1]

Preparing herself for her maiden speech to a large audience with
high expectations of raising money had not been easy. Louis Howe,
political mentor and close friend to both Eleanor and Franklin, was
all for it. He had been working to build Eleanor's interest and self-
confidence, and they had spent hours on the national vice-presidential
campaign trail talking in their train car. Her moods always registered
on her face. Howe had commanded her not to laugh when she was
nervous and to bring her voice down to a lower pitch. Now if she could
only remember his advice: "Have something to say, say it, and then
sit down." In fact, Eleanor did not know what she wanted to say, and

she was trembling with anxiety. "I did not know whether I could stand up," she later remembered.[2]

The stakes were high. Women had not yet become the ardent voters and party organizers that suffragists had hoped for, and if Miss Nancy Cook, the organizer of the program, not been so persuasive over the telephone, Eleanor would not have come at all. Perhaps she felt it was time to pay her dues—she had not decided she favored women's suffrage until Franklin came out for it. There is nothing like a second chance to get it right after failing to be part of what was a historic movement. She confessed to her girlhood friend and bridesmaid, Isabella Greenway, that sometimes she wanted to "disappear & lead a hermit's life for a year with only my husband & children & real friends to think about."[3] But that had been only a momentary reaction, which she had sometimes expressed as a wish to take a back seat—but only after she had fulfilled her obligations.

Eleanor had never made a plan for what she wanted as a wife, mother, and daughter-in-law, and her life had been unexpectedly difficult. Like her Uncle Theodore, she could be seized by dark moods, but also like him she had the energy to fight through them. Then, being in the right place—New York City—at the right time, in the 1920s, by sheer pluck she decided to act. Perhaps she had reflected on the meaning of something that Isabella had said recently about their being at an age when "it was hard to mark time" (Eleanor was thirty-seven; Isabella, thirty-five). When troubles come in youth, Isabella had written her, "we are unable to see the whole truth & have abundant strength." In older age, "we face up to it steadily and splendidly partly thro' resignation & a sense of finish." But now, Isabella observed about herself and Eleanor, "ours are the years when clear perception has come & with it the intense desire to live while we may."[4]

Eleanor and Franklin were both surprised when Eleanor developed a knack for politics and for bringing people together. Women found her easy to talk to and quickly saw her as a rising star in Democratic circles. Even some men found her easier to talk to than Franklin—she listened more intently to their ideas, and nothing seemed to surprise or offend her.

Eleanor had begun making a life for herself during World War I when she worked with other Red Cross volunteers in Washington, D.C., and discovered that she loved the physical demands of long hours in a canteen with other women. Acting on her strong sense of duty helped her to alleviate her old feelings of helplessness. The nearly eight years she and Franklin had spent in Washington while Franklin was assistant secretary of the navy had been demanding. Franklin was gone most of the time in a flurry of social rounds, and Eleanor had given birth to John, her last child. Her volunteer work was constant, but Eleanor enjoyed it. The camaraderie with other women sustained her.

Many women in the progressive campaigns of the 1920s were veterans of the suffrage and labor movements, and they knew how to work. Eleanor had met some of them in the New York City League of Women Voters and had been pleased when Esther Lape, one of the founders, and Esther's partner, Elizabeth Read, had invited her to chair the legislative committee. Elizabeth, who became Eleanor's attorney, spent time with her every week at party headquarters and at the apartment she and Esther shared in Greenwich Village, going over the *Congressional Record* to mark legislation that should be brought to the attention of league members. Eleanor, Esther, and Elizabeth were close friends for the rest of their lives. They were cut from the same cloth of upper-class New York City women with keen minds and an eagerness to embrace progressive causes together and express their own personal freedom. Nobody thought much, at least not openly, about the fact that Eleanor had been late in expressing support for women's suffrage: veteran suffragists were forgiving. Those present in the room to hear her speak for the Democratic women could say with confidence that she was now one of theirs.

•

Eleanor's work with the Democratic women was particularly important at a time when she was still trying to recover from the pain of her discovery of Franklin's infidelity. In 1918 Eleanor had been devastated by her awareness of his romance, which put distance between Eleanor and Franklin they were never able to bridge: according to their children, when their father tried to reach out physically to touch her, she rebuffed his efforts; and Eleanor never trusted him again, nor should she have—he was to break his promise never to see Lucy Mercer again. He did see her: for his presidential inaugurations, at private White House dinners, and, ultimately, in Warm Springs, where Lucy was a visitor (among others) at the time of his death. When Eleanor was summoned from Washington to Warm Springs, she discovered that Lucy had been there with Franklin, hurrying away before she arrived. Eleanor's confrontation with her daughter Anna was bitter when Anna admitted to having helped arrange her father's secret meetings with Lucy. It took a long time, but Eleanor and Anna were finally able to repair their relationship and became closer as mother and daughter. Lucy had married, giving Eleanor reason to hope, if she was looking for it, that the marriage put an end to Franklin's interests. But that was not to be the case. Although close friends like Esther Lape believed that Eleanor never stopped loving Franklin, she could not bring herself to forget.

Eleanor had reserve that saved her from retreating from the world—she had pride and could pick herself up and present a public face, especially if she had the right help. She began to trust relationships with women that she had formed through shared work. Perhaps some at the party fund-raiser in New York City had heard the Washington gossip about Lucy, an attractive daughter of a well-known family down on its luck, who needed to take a respectable job and came twice a week to help Eleanor with her correspondence. But a man's wandering affection was not unheard of in political circles, and if the gossip was true, their admiration for the way Eleanor continued to advance Franklin's name and the way Franklin was handling his life after polio may have tempered their judgment. A few years later, however, Eleanor reported in a letter to her mother-in-law news she had recently heard about Lucy: in February 1920 Lucy had married an older, wealthy widower, Winthrop Rutherfurd. Eleanor must have hoped that the marriage ended any possibility that Franklin would ever break his promise not to see Lucy again.[5]

After Franklin came down with polio, not everyone knew that he was not active in his law firm and spent weeks and months away from the city. Louis Howe kept Franklin's name on so many New York boards and in so many state political discussions that it seemed that he was already back in action. In fact, it would take Franklin most of the decade to come to terms with the realization that he was not ever going to walk again. Meanwhile, Eleanor explored her own independence, not only because Franklin had declared his but also as part of her own natural instinct for doing good.

The 1920s was a pivotal decade for both Eleanor and Franklin. The winter of 1921 had been the most difficult of Eleanor's life. Franklin had gone through periods of despondency. He needed to decide how he would live and, most of all, how to regain his optimism. After seventeen years of marriage, multiple pregnancies, the births of six children, and the unthinkable death of an infant, Eleanor undertook her own recovery from depression, a broken marriage, and a domineering mother-in-law. Franklin's suggestion that she pull herself together as he turned away from her sudden outbreaks of tears was not enough. She needed women like Esther and Elizabeth, who provided what she called "the intensive education of Eleanor Roosevelt."[6] Now she was about to meet a new friend. At Nancy Cook's fund-raiser, anyone paying close attention knew that she had stepped out on her own.

Mrs. Roosevelt did not stop to speak to the groups of women seated at the Democratic women's luncheon who reached out as she passed but walked to the center of the room and asked, "Where is Miss Cook?" Everyone knew the hardworking office secretary, and as heads turned toward her, the curly-haired, impish Nancy Cook—a "striking, crisp-haired, crisp-voiced young woman with eager eyes"—

seemed to jump forward.[7] Just as she did, Mrs. Roosevelt thrust a small bouquet of violets into her hands, a familiar symbol of affection between women. Perhaps Nan blushed, which might have made Eleanor blush. Perhaps not since the girls at Allenswood in London had filled Eleanor's room with flowers had she felt the kind of instant wave of affection that passes between female friends.

While preparing for her speech Eleanor had thought often of Allenswood's director, the electrifying Mlle. Marie Souvestre, who she said had "shocked" her into thinking for herself. Souvestre had warned her not to get caught up in the society into which her grandmother had summoned her home to make her debut. Now thirty-eight years old, Eleanor trembled but perhaps also liked it that all eyes were on her as Nan ushered her to the front of the New York ballroom. She lacked confidence, but she was not without ambition. At the front table Mrs. Sara Delano Roosevelt thrust her chin high as she turned her head to watch the other women take their seats. Her resemblance to her son was unmistakable, and the audience murmured in recognition.

Eleanor Roosevelt was certainly at home in the city—born in Manhattan, presented to New York society in a formal debut, and spending her city life in fashionable New York neighborhoods. She joined the newly formed Junior League for rich women but did her volunteer work in settlement houses. She loved all parts of the city. "Some place in New York," she once observed, "is a bit of every land on earth."[8] She went to city churches, museums, concerts, and theaters. As a child she had ridden in horse-drawn carriages, and then she found her own transport: walking and riding buses, subways, and taxis, which she liked to share with a needy rider. At first she may have been afraid of speaking, but she was not afraid of the city. Looking around at her audience, she saw kindred spirits among these progressive New Women.

As the program began, Nan stood with Eleanor at the podium, looking as if they were already good friends. The meeting unfolded so quickly that Nan later recalled the flowers Eleanor presented her, not the several thousand dollars raised. When Eleanor began traveling with Nan and sometimes her partner, Marion Dickerman, a few months later to recruit women for the Democratic Party in towns throughout New York, they were pleased to collect a ten-dollar pledge, if not the first time they knocked on a door then on a return visit. Eleanor would become a world traveler, but nothing meant more to her than those years in the 1920s when she drove her own car to many small towns and her love for the state of New York was formed. She had known the city since childhood; now she came to know the countryside around it, and she loved it.

After the meeting ended, Nan thanked people, tidied up, and hurried home to tell Marion all about it. Marion shared Nancy's excitement about the fund-raiser and agreed that the violets were an indication that Nan would see Eleanor again. Indeed, within a few weeks Eleanor invited Nan to Hyde Park, where Nan met "Granny" (Sara) and the two youngest children. Nan then was invited to bring Marion to Springwood later that summer, and it was there that they met Franklin for the first time. Soon afterward, Eleanor wrote Franklin a note, "Spent a long time with Miss Cook and agreed to get up a tea with you at once."[9] Eleanor's eagerness to get down to work inspired Esther to say of her, "The rest of us were inclined to do a good deal of theorizing. She would look puzzled and ask why we didn't do whatever we had in mind and get it out of the way."[10]

The Roosevelt family made quite an impression on both Nan and Marion, and Eleanor had a rare opportunity to bring her own friends inside the circle. It complicated relations that Marion and Nan were long-time partners: Eleanor felt that she needed to deal equally with the two of them. Marion confessed to an interviewer after Nan's death, "Eleanor cared very much more for Nan than she did for me," but declared that she felt no jealousy at all.[11] Marion, in fact, was drawn more to Franklin. She was stunned when she saw how crippled he was (she and many others had assumed that he was only lame), but she instantly found him the most charming man she had ever known.[12] She also thought that Eleanor's criticism of her mother-in-law was too harsh. Granny always seemed welcoming. Eleanor, who knew Sara far better, did not trust Sara's sincerity toward certain of Eleanor's friends who were not aristocrats. Marion and Nan were small town and middle class, and, worse than that for Sara Roosevelt's acceptance, they were bohemians—their casual dress in sweaters and knickers expressed their freedom to be themselves.

Almost at once, it seemed, Nan and "Dickie" were part of the family, both in the Roosevelt townhouse on East 65th Street and at Hyde Park, and they traveled back and forth with an ease that soon did not require a special invitation—they were expected, and they went. They were in awe of Franklin, they were keen on bringing Eleanor into the fold of Democratic New York women—never was a new recruit more promising—and they were respectful of Franklin's mother. As our story moves closer to the home that Eleanor, Marion, and Nan would share, we need to understand more about the two women who would become Eleanor's inseparable companions in the coming years.

Marion Dickerman was born 11 April 1890 in Westfield, in Oswego County, New York, the oldest of five children of Edwin Hull Dickerman and his second wife, Emily Adrienne Dickerman. The Dickermans were among the most prominent families in the Upstate New York village. They were members of the Episcopal church, where Edwin was a vestryman. For many years he served as supervisor of the town of Westfield. Other famous Westfieldians included William H. Seward, President Lincoln's secretary of state, and George M. Pullman of Pullman sleeping car fame. Mr. Dickerman, a graduate of Columbia Law School, had established a law firm in Westfield, and in 1881 he built a fine mansion and stable, where he trained his horses on a small track. Twelve years later, when Marion was a young child, he suffered financial losses that required him to move the family to what was always called the "little brown house." Marion and one sister never married. Two were teachers, and one served as a trained nurse overseas in World War I. At one point three of the sisters were living in New York City.

After attending the local public schools, Marion took her first two years of college at Wellesley. After her father died, the family could not continue to send her there, and she transferred to Syracuse University. She graduated in 1911 with a bachelor of arts degree, and the next year she earned a graduate degree in education. It was while living at a boarding house in Syracuse that Marion met Nancy Cook, a fellow student six years her senior who was engaged in graduate studies in education. They continued their studies and left together after they graduated. Within a few years Marion and Nan had taken jobs teaching at Fulton High School in Oswego County—Marion taught American history; Nan taught arts and handicrafts. Their students were sons and daughters of factory workers. Marion insisted on helping boys on court probation by making a place for them in her classroom.

When suffrage speakers came to Fulton, Marion and Nan met them and joined up with women in the town to persuade others to attend their talks. When New York became the sixth state to ratify the Nineteenth Amendment, they had reason to feel proud that they had helped make it happen. Marion and Nan were well respected in the small town, and their lives there gave them a good start to a partnership that lasted for the next half-century, sharing love, a home, political causes, friends, and work.

Although Marion and Nan were ardent pacifists, they were inspired by Woodrow Wilson's vision for peace and believed with him that World War I "was a war to end wars" to "make the world safe for democracy." After working with the Red Cross and the Liberty Loan drive, Marion and Nan were unable to find placement with the American military services, and in the spring of 1918 they applied for a British assignment in London, agreeing to do the most menial work at Endell Street Military Hospital. It was a great test not only for the skills they were to acquire but for their relationship. Marion was willing to do anything, even scrub floors, and took on nursing duties for which she had not been trained. If someone asked her to do something, she simply did it. Nancy, however, discovered that she could not do what the hospital staff expected of her, and after a week she quit.

Perhaps Marion had already helped Nan out of a difficult situation: Nan had not done well in many of her courses at Syracuse, and living with Marion had helped sustain her. Now in London Marion rescued her again, refusing to allow her to give up, urging her to find things she could do, and insisting that they stay the course. This became the pattern of their relationship. When the staff discovered that Nan knew woodworking, they assigned her to designing and making artificial limbs for the amputees. She wrote home to her father in Massena, New York, "I am in a small ward of twelve soldiers. Have a nurse and two orderlies besides myself, and a kitchen woman. All the cases are from shell wounds. . . . Not any of them will be able to ever do much again. They are all young boys, excepting two, who are men about forty-five or fifty. Our American boys will never know what other countries have suffered."[13] For more than a year Marion and Nan worked hard during the week and on weekends enjoyed the camaraderie of the mostly all-female staff. They made special friends during their hospital work who would remain close in the coming years. Nan had fewer social conquests, but she mastered woodworking, and it would become her passion in later years.

In August 1919, when the war ended and their services at Endell Hospital were no longer needed, Marion and Nan returned home. Marion's brother met her at the dock to announce that, although she was a complete novice in politics, on the basis of her good local reputation she had been selected as the Democratic Party's candidate to run against state assemblyman Thaddeus Sweet. Her brother did not think she should accept, but Marion agreed to run. Quickly turning to Nan for support, she plunged into the campaign, learning along the way. Her opponent ran a dishonest and dirty campaign. A photograph of Marion in her nurse's hat appeared in the newspaper identifying her as a nun; tires were slashed, and meeting places became suddenly unavailable. Marion kept her sense of humor and her determination. And although she lost, she took enough votes away from Thaddeus Sweet to prevent his becoming the Republican gubernatorial nominee.

Marion had made her mark as the first woman to run for the New York legislature. It was a good entry into political life. In Albany she met Al Smith during his first term as governor of New York, and she remained close to him even after Franklin Roosevelt had begun to challenge Smith's dominance of New York politics. Her relationship with Smith cooled somewhat after she met Franklin, and Marion brought to the Roosevelts her own network of political connections, many of them in labor, that proved helpful to FDR. He may have heard about her campaign against Sweet; whether he had or not, Franklin let her think so. She was no longer a novice, and her move into the Roosevelt circle was the biggest step of her life.

Following the enervating political campaign, Marion took temporary teaching and administrative jobs at New Jersey State College in Trenton and at Bryn Mawr's Summer School for Women Workers. Nan took a job in the New York City office of the Women's Division of the New York State Democratic Committee. In 1922, the same year she and Nan met Eleanor Roosevelt at the Women's Division, Marion became an instructor at the Todhunter School, a private school for daughters of wealthy residents of the Upper East Side.

Those who knew Marion described her as serious, even "mournful," her long, narrow face a match for her tall, thin body. She was not animated like Nan but rather self-contained — ladylike and composed in demeanor. "She has in repose a somewhat sorrowful countenance," an interviewer observed when Marion was in her early eighties, and that same look is reflected in photographs from her earlier years.[14] Eleanor wrote in her autobiography, *This Is My Story*, "Miss Cook and Miss Dickerman and I had become friends in just the way that Miss Lape and Miss Read and I had been first drawn together through the work we were doing. This is one of the most satisfactory ways of making and keeping friends."[15]

•

Nancy Cook was born 26 August 1884 on her father's cattle farm at the Canadian border of St. Lawrence County, New York. Her mother, Cynthia, was a homemaker. The Cooks had four children. When her father retired from farming, the family moved into the village of Massena on the Grasse River. Nan attended public schools and was always a restless student when made to sit at her desk and do work that didn't interest her—and not much book work did—but she was known for her independence. If she didn't like the lunch that was being offered at school, she ran home to eat. It wasn't far—Massena High School was on Main Street, and the Cooks' house was nearby. She did have a teacher at Massena High School whom she liked—a Miss Capp—who persuaded her that she should go to college. Nan's father thought that was a ridiculous idea, or so she later remembered; Massena should have plenty to interest her. The village was on a big shipping lane on the great St. Lawrence River, and there was much to see.

Mr. Cook was a self-made man who had come to Massena as a teenager to work in a blacksmith shop. Within a few years he owned his own shop and thereafter began to acquire farmland. He bought and sold a large number of farms before retiring and moving back into town. Nan had a lot of respect for her father, as did others in Massena, but she was always looking for ways to escape boredom.

After graduating from high school Nan bought her first camera and began taking photographs of local sites. She turned the photos into the first picture postcards sold in Massena stores. Thus began her lifelong interest in photography, and she made enough money selling her cards to pay for college. She applied to Syracuse University and was accepted. She entered the art school, but she and her teachers soon determined that she wasn't really an artist and that she belonged in education. She transferred to the Teachers' College, where Dean Jacob Richard Street, a Canadian who had joined the faculty at Syracuse in 1900, took a special interest in her. She excelled, and after graduating in 1915 she was invited back to take charge of the work in the summer school. It was during this time that she met Harriet May Mills, a Syracuse native and leading suffragist.

Mills was a tireless worker who traveled all over New York State to organize the suffrage movement. She brought Carrie Chapman Catt to Syracuse, and Nan quickly became caught up in the movement for women's suffrage. Teaching seemed dull by comparison, and she lacked the patience needed to teach adolescent students. Politics drew her, and she was a good organizer. She had a lot to tell Marion when they returned to their boarding house each evening, and by the time they graduated the two women were committed partners and suffragists.

It was after teaching a few years at Fulton High School in Fulton, New York, that Nan and Marion had gone to London to work in the Endell Street Military Hospital, which was staffed almost entirely by women, including a woman surgeon. Nan became indispensable there when she learned to make prostheses for the amputees, but she did not make good friends as easily as Marion. Marion had a capacity to adapt to new people and new ideas, whereas Nan seemed to see insults and rifts with others that Marion ignored. But together they made an indomitable and harmonious pair. Although Nan was older, Marion was the mother hen. By the time peace was declared in 1918, Nan and Marion were ready to return home. Although Marion inevitably lost her bid for the New York legislature, both women nevertheless felt that the campaign had been worth the effort to show what women could do, even against an entrenched male politician. Marion continued in education, but Nan had been bitten by the politics bug.

When Harriet May Mills asked Nan to come to New York to be her assistant in the Women's Division of the New York State Democratic Committee, Nan gladly went. After Harriet retired, Nan took over the office, which she would run for nineteen years. Marion continued to pick up teaching jobs until she could find employment in New York City and join Nan in an apartment in Greenwich Village.

•

Now that women had received the right to vote, there was a lot of fieldwork to be done. Eleanor and Nan immediately began strategizing with Caroline O'Day, a New Yorker and wealthy widow who was working in the Democratic Party Women's Division, about the best way to organize women voters in the state. For the next several years Eleanor, Marion, Nan, and Elinor Morgenthau, who was also active in the League of Women Voters and the New York State Democratic Women's Division, traveled together, making contacts and helping develop the local chapters. Caroline would later benefit from this network—she was elected four times to Congress—and the women's efforts also gave FDR a network of contacts and a cadre of workers for his own political future.

The sight of Franklin struggling in 1921 to walk down the avenue from Springwood to the gates was disheartening, but Marion trusted that he would overcome his difficulties. She believed in him and wanted to be part of his future. Eleanor was beginning to have ambitions of her own. It was ingrained in her to demean her own efforts— a defense if she failed and a show of female modesty (a woman should be modest)—but those who came to know her best understood that Eleanor had a good deal of self-interest. She began to have her own ideas about how government could serve the needs of the people, and she showed signs of being a good politician.

After the summer of 1922 Nan and Marion were Eleanor's most intimate friends. When the Roosevelts moved back to the city, the children returned to their private schools and Franklin saw various doctors about his legs, and Eleanor went on the road with Marion, Nan, Elinor Morgenthau, and Caroline O'Day, who had succeeded Harriet May Mills as chairman of the Women's Division of the state Democratic Party. They traveled in all kinds of weather, dealing with flat tires, running out of gas, and failing to find anyone at home when they called on individuals who might help. They stayed in modest lodges and talked to anyone who would listen, and their perseverance paid off. By the spring of 1924 they had organized all but five New York counties.

Politics was also fun. In the fall of 1924 the Singing Teapot, a seven-passenger touring car, left New York City promptly at noon carrying members of the Women's Division for a two-week tour of the state to win votes for Al Smith, who was running for reelection as governor of New York against Theodore Roosevelt Jr. The news reporter for the *Ogdensburg Republican-Journal*, following protocol in calling women by their father's or husband's names, noted that one of the drivers of the car was Miss Anna Eleanor Roosevelt, daughter of Mr. and Mrs. Franklin D. Roosevelt. Among the other drivers were Miss Emily Smith, daughter of Governor and Mrs. Smith, and Miss Ella O'Day of Rye, daughter of Caroline O'Day, respectively associate state chairman and chairman of the Women's Division. The Buick Company donated the car for the occasion; Mrs. Henry (Elinor) Morgenthau Jr. paid the expenses. Among the passengers were Mrs. J. Borden Harriman of New York and Washington, representing the national ticket, and Miss Harriet May Mills, Syracuse, representing Governor Smith.

The Buick touring car had been outfitted on the top with a paper replica of a teapot, which steamed as it arrived in towns from New York City to Buffalo and swung through the southern part of the state to remind gawkers about the Teapot Dome oil scandals of Warren G. Harding's Republican administration. Nothing was too challenging for the women during this excursion. Local chairs met them at each location. In Potsdam they attended a street meeting at 8:30 p.m. and left the next morning for Canton at 10:00 a.m. and a thirty-minute stop at Gouverneur.

Those who knew Eleanor Roosevelt appreciated that she kept a tight schedule. But perhaps even they were surprised that she had unleashed her imagination to help defeat her cousin Theodore, thereby widening the bitter divide between the Oyster Bay Roosevelts and the Hyde Park branch of the family, who were upstaging them. The friends themselves had a whole lot of fun, although years later Eleanor was obliged to admit that the Teapot Tour had been a "rough stunt."[16] But she did not offer an apology.

•

In the election of 1924 Eleanor made a valiant effort to get more women represented in Democratic Party decisions, but in the end she and her cohorts were denied access to the all-male committees running the show. Her leadership had been exceptional, however, and she had made a name for herself; so had Franklin, who had agreed to nominate Governor Smith for president at the party's convention in Madison Square Garden. It marked his first public appearance after polio, and many historians have emphasized the importance of the occasion for him. Sara, Eleanor, Marion, Nan, and four of the Roosevelt children were seated in the balcony when the drama began. The convention delegates watched Roosevelt's perilous approach to the podium on the arm of his son James. Once there, he triumphantly positioned himself and to thunderous applause gave what became known as the "Happy Warrior" speech. The speech borrowed that phrase from a Wordsworth poem to describe Smith, but the audience understood that it best applied to Roosevelt himself. Smith lost the nomination to a compromise candidate, John W. Davis, a Wall Street lawyer, and continued as New York governor. FDR was the real winner. Eleanor was wary about what it meant for her.

When Franklin returned to the family's New York City apartment after the convention, Marion came to the house to congratulate him and was told that he wanted to see her in his upstairs bedroom. When she walked into his room, he was sitting up in bed beaming. "Marion, I did it!" he exclaimed.[17] It was the first of several times when Franklin invited Marion personally to share his political triumphs. And it was one of many times that Franklin relied on Marion and Nan. As Frances Perkins, who worked in FDR's administration when he was New York governor and later when he was president, as his U.S. secretary of labor, observed when Franklin was governor of New York, Marion, Nan, and Caroline O'Day "were women that he saw all the time. He didn't have to go out on the highways and by ways" to seek advice.[18]

In 1928 Eleanor again worked for Smith's presidential campaign. Although she did not campaign for Franklin, who was considering running for governor in the same election, she encouraged him, thus, observers thought, making the difference in Franklin's decision. Eleanor had persuaded Franklin to take a call from Smith asking him to run, and Franklin agreed to Smith's request despite the opposition of his secretary and now his constant companion, Marguerite "Missy" LeHand. Franklin won and Smith lost. Eleanor was more disheartened by Smith's defeat than she was pleased by Franklin's victory. Marion and Nan were elated.

As Eleanor became more politically active, letters about her flew back and forth among the Oyster Bay Roosevelt relatives, none harsher than one from a source that must have been a stab in the heart for Eleanor: her beloved Auntie Bye, who had encouraged Grandmother Hall to send Eleanor to Allenswood. Writing to her sister Corinne, Bye snidely lamented, as possibly only a family member could, about the effects politics was having on Eleanor: "Alas and lackaday! Since politics have become her choicest interest all her charm has disappeared, and the fact is emphasized by the companions she chooses to bring with her."[19] Eleanor and Nan had shown up at Bye's house wearing identical outfits of knickerbockers, which were, in fact, quite stylish; it was Bye whose love for the latest fashion had stopped when she was too old and infirm to command her own audience. The Oyster Bay relatives would have been equally appalled to hear about Eleanor's arrest for disorderly conduct when she and Marion joined a protest strike of women workers in New York City in the winter of 1926. Eleanor was developing public concerns and personal courage that would carry her through a lifetime of activism, and a cadre of women friends would be ready to go with her.

Eleanor thought that there was nothing unusual about sharing a cottage with two women recognized as partnered in an intimate domestic life. She already knew the pleasures of a shared life modeled by Esther Lape and Elizabeth Read, whose apartment in Greenwich Village provided her with escapes from the twin Roosevelt townhouses on the Upper East Side (Eleanor and Franklin's was next to Mama's). Eleanor could create such a domestic setting for herself with Marion and Nan. For their part, Marion and Nan likely discussed with one another what privacy they might be giving up in sharing a home and a life with a married woman who had a large family. The fact that living at Val-Kill put them close to Franklin was perhaps as great an advantage for them as being Eleanor's housemates, because Marion and Nan were keenly absorbed in Franklin's career and shared Eleanor's determination to help him return to public life. Although hundreds of friends visited the Roosevelts at Springwood, none had easier access than Marion and Nan. The time seemed right for them to take the next step. After fourteen years of being together they were ready for a new adventure. It was the beginning of the most significant and exciting chapter in their lives.

3

THE DECISION TO BUILD THE COTTAGE

Why shouldn't you three have a cottage here of your own? — Franklin Roosevelt

On the late summer afternoon in 1924 when the decision was made to build a cottage on the banks of Fall-Kill Creek about two miles east of the Big House, Franklin, Eleanor, Marion, and Nan were in close harmony, having spent the weekend together at Springwood and having celebrated the end of the summer season with a picnic in one of their favorite places. We imagine that the afternoon may have unfolded something like this.

Eleanor, Marion, and Nan had walked the two miles from Springwood through woods and farmland to Fall-Kill Creek to meet Franklin, who had been driven there by one of his men along with his sons Franklin Jr. ("Brud") and John, for the last weekend picnic of the season. The men and boys laughed as the car bounced over the rutted roads and the makeshift bridge. They were already at their favorite site when the three women arrived arm in arm. As excited as their father to be free and outdoors, Brud and John raced toward the water's edge to work on their fort in the marsh.

Franklin's man picked him up and carried him to the hill above the pond, Franklin joking about the weight he had gained since he had been exercising with his lady therapist. Franklin always tried to make it easier on those who saw how helpless he was by making lots of jokes. When the women arrived — Franklin called them "our gang" — Marion reached into the backseat for the blanket and hurried to spread it out for him. Eleanor took out the picnic baskets, and Nan scratched in the old ashes to lay a new fire. A startled frog splashed into the water, and in the nearby woods there were sounds of birds; in the distance a farmer was working in a field. It was a cool afternoon, the summer heat already fading, and there was some yellow in the scrubby trees, but the dominant color was the blue of the sky. By the time hot dogs were cooked on the spits and potato salad was added to the plates and cold drinks had been passed around, Franklin was in fine form, continuing last night's stories about riding his horse over these same fields with his father. After the picnic had been put away, the boys raced back to their fort, Franklin stretched out in the waning sun, and the three women took a long walk through the woods, Eleanor setting the pace.

When the women returned, a chill had settled over the water and Franklin was talking to his tenant, Moses Smith, who rented a house and farm called Woodlawns on the Val-Kill estate and raised vegetables, chickens, and cows. Moses was also a good friend, and the two men often discussed local agricultural issues. Today Moses had come to talk about some newly planted trees. Franklin was worried about them. All in all, he would have preferred fewer picnics and more rain. He asked Moses to keep an eye on the trees because he would be leaving soon to join some friends on a Florida houseboat they had rented to motor about the Intracoastal Waterway, get in some fishing, and soak up some sun. Although it was a false hope, Franklin believed that the sun and water would restore full strength to his useless legs. He could still wrestle with his sons, and he liked to show off his upper body strength by dropping from a chair and dragging himself up the stairs. Here by the Fall-Kill he was content to eat and laugh and entertain Marion and Nan, who encouraged him with their questions.

In later years Marion reminisced about the first time they had been leaving the Big House with Eleanor to go on a picnic and Nan had gone in to kiss Franklin goodbye. He had pretended to weep, "Oh, I want to go, too!"[1] The women readily agreed, and he laughed and joked with them all the way.

Now on the creek bank on that fall afternoon Eleanor lamented that this would be their last picnic of the season. Marion and Nan nodded. And whether or not they had already talked about it—there is no record of it in Marion's memories of that day—this last picnic seemed to be on everyone's mind. Marion and Nan and Eleanor and Franklin all exchanged thoughtful looks.

Whether the idea had been planned or was a sudden inspiration, when the women looked toward him, Franklin spoke (Marion recalled his words even at the end of her life), "But aren't you girls silly? This isn't Mother's land. I bought this acreage myself. And why shouldn't you three have a cottage here of your own, so you could come and go as you please?"[2] Their surprise and delight were immediate, expressed in a sudden burst of energy as they nodded. With some nervous chatter they began to load up the baskets and carry them to the car. Eleanor called to the boys, and they ran back like rabbits. Clearly, Franklin had set something in motion that would change the way they all lived. He was not of a mind to say so, but perhaps it was his gift to Eleanor.

When the women arrived back at the Big House, Franklin was seated in the library with his mother, who did not take her eyes from her son when they entered the room. He was explaining something about the Florida houseboat, and she did not look pleased. Mama did not invite them to sit by the fire, and they hesitated, unsure what to do. Outside the river flowed and night came to the valley.

Remember this — the old bridge, the hillside, the marshes, and the creek ran clear and cold.

4

THE FAMILY VACATION

Things were generally "rough and ready." There were no cucumber or watercress sandwiches or dainty things! —Ellie Roosevelt Seagraves

After the decision was made to build the cottage at Fall-Kill Creek, Franklin urged Eleanor, Marion, and Nan to take the boys to the family house on Campobello Island in New Brunswick, Canada, and turn over the supervision of the construction to him. He had long wanted his children to enjoy Campobello as much as he had when he was young. His father and mother had first taken him to the island when he was only two, and until the fateful trip in 1921 when he was struck down by polio, he had gone every summer, becoming an expert sailor and exploring every inch of what he called his "beloved island." (Indeed, he would not return to Campobello until 1933, when he came on a U.S. Navy vessel as president of the United States.) In a sense, Marion and Nan would serve as his proxies on Campobello. While the family was away, Franklin would have a project he would enjoy immensely because he fancied himself something of an architect; he took Thomas Jefferson and Monticello as his ideal. And it would focus his mind, requiring attention to details but still allowing him to send instructions from afar—wherever he was trying to find another kind of treatment for his paralysis.

After Eleanor, Marion, and Nan agreed to take the younger boys and their friends to the Roosevelt cottage on Campobello, they planned the long trip that they would make every summer until 1929, when they took their grand tour of Europe instead. They would camp along the way, pitching tents at night, with the three women sleeping in one tent and the boys in a pup tent nearby. Nan was to prepare all their meals on a camp stove.

Eleanor grasped the opportunity to be more present in the lives of Brud and John than she had in those of her three older children, all of whom were beginning to show signs of discontent. Franklin was no longer able to be the physically active father they once enjoyed, and Eleanor was always on the go. She had come to rely on Nan and Marion for help with the younger boys. On weekends in New York City Eleanor, Marion, and Nan had taken them to all the popular sites—the museums, the Statue of Liberty, the waterfront, Central Park. When Franklin expressed a desire that the boys learn to swim, the three women took swimming lessons at the New York YWCA in preparation. Marion especially wanted to get to know the children and helped them with their lessons. In time she became a go-between when Eleanor's tolerance for the boys' perceived misbehavior wore thin.

With Nan and Marion along, the trip would be a delightful adventure for Eleanor. Not only had she found friends for herself; she had also found helpmates for the children—Nancy with her skills for cooking and camping out, Marion with her skills for managing rambunctious boys.

•

Campobello had been a popular summer resort for wealthy families from the Northeast since the middle to late 1800s. In the days before World War I families came and stayed for the entire summer. In late summer or early fall the summer people packed up and left, leaving their staffs to close up the houses, take in the wicker chairs from the porches, collect the lamps for winter repairs, clean out the fireplaces, and close the shutters, returning the island to the locals, who fished and cooked and told stories during the long winter days and nights. The families who came to the island for the summer provided work for most of the island's men and women, but the locals knew the difference: at St. Anne's Anglican Church the Roosevelts and other wealthy families occupied the center pews while the islanders sat on the sides. The summer people were nevertheless an important source of income in the island's economy.

Before the Roosevelt International Bridge was opened in 1962, there was no easy way to reach the remote island. Summer families arriving in the late 1800s to stay at the Tyn-y-Coed and Tyn-y-Maes hotels faced a long journey by train and boat. In the summer of 1921, when Sara Delano Roosevelt arrived home from England, having been told that Franklin was ill and anxious to reach Campobello, she traveled by train from New York, changing in Boston and at Ayers Junction, Massachusetts, to make the last part of the journey on a single railcar pulled by a tiny wood-burning engine to Eastport, Maine, where a boat met her and carried her to the island.[1] Even today, with easy automobile travel and bridge access, the trip to Campobello is a long drive.

•

Eleanor, seasoned by moving her large family from New York City to Hyde Park several times a year, was masterful at getting them to Campobello every summer, with a lot of help from an entourage— often she brought along a tutor and one or more governesses. At the end of her life Eleanor had become known as one of the most traveled women in American history. Perhaps it is not too much to say that she learned a great deal about how to manage travels during all her summers going to and from Campobello. Sometimes she would stay there only a few weeks, return home, and then come back to be with family or visitors. Her stamina often tested Marion's and Nan's.

Perhaps the most dramatic change on Campobello Island since Eleanor's first visit in 1904 was in Eleanor herself. She had first come as a shy girl courted by her ebullient cousin and carefully watched by his mother. Sara was less observant than a next-door neighbor, who saw the couple falling in love and told Sara that she was making arrangements in her will for Sara to buy her house for Franklin and Eleanor, which Sara did in 1909. Eleanor delighted in rearranging the furniture in every room to suit her. It was her first chance to be her own interior decorator.

Eleanor recorded other important personal dates in Campobello as well. In 1914 she miscalculated her due date and unexpectedly gave birth to her fourth child, Franklin Jr. In 1918 she was there alone with the children and her staff, wondering about the reason for Franklin's long delay in joining the family. Why was he spending so much time boating on the Potomac (along with others, it was Lucy Mercer's name that leapt out)? In the summer of 1917 she worried about being in Campobello without him and urged him to join them. In his letter to her, he chided her for accusing him of not wanting to join them, calling her a "goosey girl."[2] Then she discovered the love letters from Lucy to Franklin that confirmed her suspicions, and she confronted him with the evidence. The crisis passed, the marriage was preserved, but the damage was done. In late August on the island in 1921 Franklin was stricken with polio. He was thirty-nine years old. So many unhappy memories, and yet here she was, going back in 1925 with Marion and Nan and the boys, hoping for a different experience. They set out to drive the seven-passenger Buick north along the Hudson, Lake George, Lake Champlain, and on into Canada, and then down through New Hampshire and across Maine to Campobello.

Now that Eleanor had a touring car and could share the driving with Marion and Nan, they got to know the New England road map as never before. Eleanor was intensely drawn to the natural landscape, and en route to Campobello Island she, Marion, and Nan had time to take in the beauties of northeastern rural life. The trip reaffirmed the women's conviction that the woods and water of Val-Kill would give them the inspiration they needed to prepare for the next phase of their lives.

•

We learn a lot about how well we get along with others when we travel with them. Apparently for the three women the only wrinkle in the long car trip was the high energy of the young boys—together with Brud and John they had George Draper Jr., the son of FDR's doctor, and Henry Roosevelt, the son of Eleanor's younger brother, Hall. Brud and John got into various scrapes and accidents along the way that were especially unsettling to their mother. Eleanor had been nervous about taking the boys in the first place, unsure that she could manage, but Marion and Nan reassured her, Franklin wanted them to go, and the boys were excited.

Camping en route to the island proved a unique experience for all of them. They stayed in primitive sites, heated coffee in a frying pan, and ate under the stars before turning in for the night. Once a landowner turned them away from his fields, saying that he did not want the kind of women who traveled without their husbands camping there. They moved on. The air grew lighter as they traveled closer to the sea.

Of special pleasure were the stopovers to visit relatives and friends, particularly Mary ("Molly") Dewson, the head of the Women's Division of the Democratic National Committee, and her partner, Polly Porter, who spent their summers in Castine, Maine. The overnight at Moss Acre, their summer home in Castine, was to be the last before the final leg of the motor trip to Campobello. By the time they reached Castine, the Maine landscape had imprinted itself upon Eleanor's imagination, and her thoughts had turned to Sarah Orne Jewett's *Country of the Pointed Firs*. Eleanor was with her best friends, who were helping her relax her strict rules for the two little fellows she wanted to learn to mother.

The little town of Castine on Penobscot Bay glowed in the midday light, and the great, welcoming home of Molly and Polly beckoned them as they rolled down the long driveway. The rural landscape was a reminder of the setting they would come home to at Val-Kill at summer's end. Dogs barked and leapt and were shushed by Polly, while Molly reached for the bags. As the boys piled out of the car and started scuffling, Eleanor tried to quiet them, but Marion merely laughed and shooed them away. There was an ease in the way the women held hands and leaned into one another. Molly and Eleanor immediately started talking New York Democratic politics. The others disappeared into the back of the house, where a cook had left supper on the wood stove. Molly and Eleanor sat down in front of the fire in the large living room that looked toward the bay.

After a while, the women all took a walk to bring provisions for the boys, who had gone to a cabin by the shore, and then returned to the house for a nap. And when everyone was rested they gathered on the wide, shady porch. After another hour or so, supper. More hours passed in laughter and conversation, and before they all went to their rooms to close the windows, they stood together in the near-dark and watched light disappear over the water. Eleanor had promised the boys that she was going to sleep with them in the small rustic cabin, and off she went to the shore. Down below, the boys had quieted. As Eleanor walked to join them she had reason to feel that she was beginning to master life at last.

The next morning Eleanor and the boys straggled up to the house for breakfast (sausage, syrup, pancakes), and then they all hugged one another in farewell — the boys escaping the kisses — and the travelers were once more on their way. Another stop for extra provisions and then on to Lubec, which smelled of fish, for a simple lunch at one of those small places of local renown found on every coast, and a hearty welcome from the owner. Time was of the essence — they must arrive before 5 p.m. or miss the boat — so there were constant reminders to hurry, hurry. Then they all piled into the ferry for the trip across the Narrows, found their sea legs on the choppy water, and, landing, stepped off and steadied themselves on the slippery dock. The boys were fearless, "made of rubber," their father had laughed, and it made them feel good to think they were. A few local men came down to help them up the hill with their bags. Before mounting the steps to the porch of the Roosevelt cottage, the women, a little breathless, turned back for a last look at the shore that now seemed to all but disappear. The sound of the sea birds, the East Quoddy Lighthouse, and the fog blowing in at night were familiar: Eleanor was home, and Marion and Nan experienced with her what home could mean. Accustomed to far less comfort during their travels, Marion and Nan luxuriated in the thirty-five-room "cottage" on an island with dramatic sunsets, scenic walks, and boating expeditions (with meals packed for the occasions), in the company of a large family the two of them could call their own.

Tomorrow, Eleanor announced, they would pick blueberries. Eleanor had first picnicked on the island in the summer of 1904, when she was secretly engaged to Franklin. Over the years, entertaining guests with a picnic had become a Roosevelt signature. The same informal manner of eating out-of-doors would later prevail at Val-Kill: baskets would disgorge quantities of food until the children were satisfied and had gone off to their mysterious games, and the adults walked or lay back in the sun and listened to silence broken only by bird calls, and sometimes by the clang of a buoy, and sometimes a murmur of contentment from the gang.

The women unpacked, talked, laughed, complained a little about their aches and pains after the long trip, caught up with the neighbors, sent word by post to Castine that they had arrived (there was no telephone), tested the lamps (already filled, the wicks trimmed), ate a light meal, and lit the fires that had been laid for them. In no time the boys, promised a sail the next morning with Captain Calder, were asleep in their beds.

Sailing picnics were a favorite entertainment at Campobello. Eleanor's granddaughter Nina Roosevelt (Gibson), John and Anne Clark Roosevelt's daughter, remembered, "Our picnics often were on the fishing boat while we were fishing or watching whales that came into the bay in August.... Somehow the hot dogs tasted best on the open water and the smell of the charcoal grill which was placed on the stern of the boat gave off that lovely cozy feeling of a fire at home on a cold wintry day."[3] Eleanor "Ellie" or "Sistie" (Seagraves), Eleanor's first grandchild, Anna's daughter, remembered that nothing was fancy about her grandmother's picnics—"There were no cucumber or watercress sandwiches or dainty things! Things were generally 'rough and ready' for the period, especially if in an open, informal location, such as the beach at Campobello, or around the pool at Hyde Park."[4]

Before the local women who had been there to greet them and look after them left for the day, Eleanor met with them to ask about their families and their needs. "She is one of us," they always reported to inquisitive strangers. And of course they knew Franklin, a native son loved by the islanders since he was a boy on a sailboat. That is the way they liked to think of him, not the way it was when they had stood back and watched him carried out of the house on a stretcher, struck down by that dread disease, polio. He did not come anymore. When Eleanor returned without him, she always brought friends. "There are good and bad memories there," she reflected, "but the bad get the better of me when I'm there alone.... There the night has a thousand eyes."[5]

•

Now Eleanor's time begins. Campobello gives her a sense of rest. She knits and reads by the fire. Between the mainland and the island the great tides rise and fall, dividing her world. Peace comes. On 18 July Eleanor writes in her journal, "We marked our first towels."[6] The linens, monogrammed E M N, are for the new cottage on the Val-Kill. Tonight Eleanor might read to her friends from her favorite book, *Death Comes for the Archbishop*, by the American novelist Willa Cather, a story of friendship. Since her school days at Allenswood near London she has loved to read aloud—and she reads slowly, the perfect pace for the story of Father Vaillant and Bishop Latour, two French priests sent to serve in the vast, unruly new American territory of New Mexico. She lingers over descriptions of the Southwest, where she had been an enchanted traveler herself once with Franklin on a visit to see her dear friend Isabella Greenway and Isabella's family. There is so much that she appreciates in the priests' story. It is a story of courage and loneliness and the loyalty of friendship. No book speaks more intimately to her heart.

Eleanor has heard that Miss Cather has a place on the next island over, Grand Manan, and she has often wished she could meet her. Perhaps she has heard that Miss Cather does not like to be interrupted. Eleanor understands that, though she herself would never turn anyone away. Sometimes she has stood on the crescent of Herring Cove and looked across the Bay of Fundy to Grand Manan and wondered what an artist does all day. Nan has helped Eleanor understand how imagination works and has filled her with respect for what Nan can make with her own talented hands. Eleanor may suspect that Miss Cather, a conservative lady, would dislike her liberal views, but if that is true, Eleanor would tolerate their differences.

Eleanor looks at her friends seated around her and begins reading: "One summer evening in the year 1848 three Cardinals and a missionary Bishop from America were dining together in the gardens of a villa in the Sabine hills overlooking Rome." Nan and Marion smile at one another. The story is set in motion: Jean Marie Latour, stimulated by his recent seminary studies, is going to be sent to the new vicariate in New Mexico, where he will travel with his friend Joseph Vaillant. Jean and Joseph are often separated by their visits to remote and dangerous places to deliver the sacraments, and at those times each lives mostly in solitude. They save up much to say to each other during their times together, and their reunions are always cherished.

Eleanor pauses, adds a log to the fire, and thinks. A determination to try new things will be her most enduring quest. Her friends watch her closely because of late she has begun to show signs of letting down her reserve. The story of the priestly comrades casts warmth over the friends seated in front of the fire. Eleanor loves Cather's world, which she has described to Marion and Nan from her own travels in the Southwest—the pueblos, the pinyon logs burning in the fireplace, the Indian blankets covering earthen floors or hung on the walls like tapestries, and the shrines. Eleanor and Marion and Nan have talked of having just such a home, with a fireplace and a colorful Indian blanket and white stucco walls that will frame their cottage on Fall-Kill Creek.

The fire has settled and her friends are nodding off, Marion's long face as composed and solemn as a priest's. Eleanor smiles and says it is almost time to go to bed. But she will send them off with one final scene. She gives the old priest Jean Latour the last words: "The Miracles of the Church seem to me to rest not so much upon faces or voices or healing power coming suddenly near to us from afar off, but upon our perceptions being made finer, so that for a moment our eyes can see and our ears can hear what there is about us always." She closes the book.

Eleanor stands at the window and looks across the glittering water toward Lubec. It seems to her like the ghost of Mont St. Michel — a place she will one day see with Marion and Nan and the boys — where the great tides that sweep in *à la vitesse d'un cheval au galop* are as severe as those in the Bay of Fundy. She thinks of the legend of the Archangel Michael appearing before the bishop and instructing him to build a church on the rocky isle. She thinks of Cather's story of the Mexican peasant's humble vision of the Virgin Mary and of the shrine to honor Our Lady of Guadalupe. And she feels that she herself is beginning some pilgrimage of her own, searching for the greatest of miracles, sanctuary.

As the Campobello night ends, the friends mount the stairs to their beds, hands holding to the banister in the dim light. The lamps are turned down, the fire is banked.

The next morning Eleanor, Marion, and Nan feel at one with one another and with the great outdoors. They continue their discussion of the cottage going up on the Fall-Kill, what it will look like, how they will use the rooms, how they will walk the trails and listen to the creek. They warm to the thought of the life they will make together.

5

THE LOVE NEST

. . . the birds chirping everywhere. — Marion Dickerman

Once it was agreed that a cottage would be built at the Fall-Kill and that Franklin would supervise the construction, Franklin and Nan began talking with the architect Henry Toombs — Caroline O'Day's cousin — whose Val-Kill design would be the first of several important projects he would work on with Franklin: the James Roosevelt Memorial Library in Hyde Park; the post offices at Poughkeepsie and Rhinebeck; Franklin's cottages at Warm Springs; and Top Cottage at Val-Kill. Indeed, the handprint of Franklin Roosevelt would be seen all over the valley. Franklin had good reason to think of himself as the historian of Hyde Park.

While Eleanor, Marion, and Nan were with the boys in Campobello, Franklin took care of getting the cottage under way. His letters to the women described the progress: excavating for the swimming pool, ordering lumber and lawn seed, and dealing with merchants in Poughkeepsie and elsewhere. Some of the plans for the cottage contained his notations, which delighted him.

When historians record that FDR built a cottage for Eleanor and her friends, readers have reason to assume that he paid for it. His mother, after all, had built a house for him and his family next to hers on East 65th Street, paid the costs, and held the deed. But in fact, Eleanor, Marion, and Nan, although with more limited resources, shared equally in the costs of building the cottage, and they owned it together. Eleanor had an inheritance from her family, and Marion and Nan had been earning salaries for most of a decade and living modestly; they were prepared to invest their savings. Marion later said that, though she and Nan had less, they always wanted to do their part.

As to whose idea it was to build the cottage, Marion said it was Franklin's, in a story historians have repeated with only slight variation as to his exact words. Maybe it happened just that way, but Marion was adroit at handling Franklin and willing to give him credit for most things. He had a keen awareness of ownership—as soon as he proposed that they build a cottage, he reminded them that he owned the property and could do what he wanted to with it without asking Mama; he would give them a lifetime lease to about eight acres. He did not say he would pay for constructing the cottage, or that he would own it.

Franklin was an acquisitive fellow. He loved buying up the property around Springwood, which belonged to his mother and would come to him only at her death. In 1911 he had bought the large Bennett Farm with a house and 194 acres at a cost of $10,000. The farm was divided almost in half by Fall-Kill Creek, and a particular site along the banks had become the family's favorite picnic site. Franklin had primitive roads cut from the Big House to Val-Kill so that when he began driving again in 1926 (in a car with hand controls) he could have a sense of freedom, out of sight of the parallel exercise bars he had installed on the front lawn at Springwood and the avenue from the Big House to the road, where he struggled to walk with crutches.

Regardless of whose idea it was to build the cottage at Val-Kill, all agreed that it made sense: they all enjoyed the picnics, Sara closed up the Big House for the winter when there were still weekends they could enjoy in Hyde Park, Franklin owned the property— why not build a cottage! Several months later Franklin and the three women signed a legal agreement that the property would revert to Franklin's estate at the women's deaths. Even before the legal papers were signed, the foundation had been dug and the future was in sight. Franklin, who had been swimming in the indoor pools of neighbors, was especially eager to divert the creek to make a small swimming hole near the cottage.

It is possible that Eleanor, Marion, and Nan had already been discussing owning a place together before that late-summer picnic when it was decided. They had become a threesome, working in women's politics in New York; sharing responsibilities for the children, especially the two youngest boys; and traveling together from their respective houses in the city for weekends at Hyde Park. In her first autobiography, *This I Remember*, Eleanor does not say how the idea originated: she merely says that Franklin "helped to design and build a stone cottage." She acknowledges that Franklin chose the style (Dutch colonial), the architect (Henry Toombs), and the contractor (Henry Clinton). It was Franklin's decision to use as much fieldstone for the walls and chimneys as could be harvested from old walls on his property, pulled out of the fields with horses.

If the women had wanted to choose their own design, they would have had to stand up to Franklin, which they may not have been ready to do. But perhaps they had no reason to object to Franklin's ideas. And why would they? It is likely that the planned fieldstone walls and chimneys appealed as much to them as to Franklin—both Marion and Nan had grown up in traditional two-story clapboard houses reflective of middle-class Victorian taste in small Upstate New York towns. In building a house of their own, the women could put down roots in the Hudson Valley they all loved in a house that reflected the region's particular history and geography.

Franklin made building decisions, but Nan insisted on keeping her hand on the design. She was the first to make drawings for the cottage, and she made a wooden model of it. Toombs did not like her preliminary sketches but apparently was satisfied that he could work with her. They sometimes thought of themselves as partners in design over Franklin's objections. Nan and Toombs had agreed to place a large Palladian window in the main room but withdrew their suggestion when Franklin said it was not Dutch colonial and if the window was there he would not visit the house. They heard the threat, whether exaggerated or serious, and a chimney with a big fireplace took the place of the window. Franklin also voted down dormer windows.

The preliminary plan for the cottage, dated 7 May 1925, lists the structure as a "residence for Miss Nancy Cook & Miss Marion Dickerman Hyde Park, New York."[1] The absence of Eleanor's name suggests that she was not present onsite when the plan was submitted; the house by signed agreement belonged to the three of them. Although Eleanor often differed with Franklin in the design details, she trusted Marion and Nan to represent her interests with him. That was not always easy. Franklin was by turns playful and willful, and the women had to learn how to negotiate with him. They took for granted that they had no need to negotiate with one another.

A recently discovered six-page letter from Marion to Franklin in a box of FDR's receipts highlights her relationship to the family. The letter was handwritten on Marion and Nan's stationery at 1271 West 12th Street, New York City, and it was sent to Franklin, who was in Warm Springs with Missy LeHand.[2]

> Sunday [early spring 1925]
> Dear Franklin,
> Indeed we needed you on Saturday when Eleanor, Nan, Elliott, the two little boys [Franklin Jr. and John] and I went up to Hyde Park for that was the day that Mr. Brown [unidentified] meet [sic] us there. He was enchanted with the spot which was charming for the sun was warm, the buds just beginning to swell and the birds chirping everywhere. Mr. Brown said at once, "The living room must face south; the axis of the house is all wrong, that tree should be the determining point," etc., many, many ideas and most of them excellent ones. The poor house however has been quite abruptly changed so as to almost face south; there is again a tiny cellar and a hot air furnace. A whole new set of plans must be done and Henry [Toombs] is working on them this week so perhaps we will be sending them to you in about a week.
> I am enclosing a picture of the car [which E M N shared]. . . . It is much "better than it looks" in the picture but it was hard to take indoors. The other picture is to show you how high the brook is. We want to put in a little, tiny dam so as to keep it most as high for it is fascinating.

Later we motored to Beacon where Nan and I were to take the train to New York and the rest were to go to Newburgh but the "Cadillac" behaved so badly that we reached the station only to see the train pulling out. I couldn't miss it for it was my brother's birthday and I was due home for dinner so we ran. It sounds absurd but between the kindness of the brakeman, a friendly engineer and one or two others we reached the train, climbed up on the rear car and with a drier throat than you have ever seen sank into our seats with a fair prayer for "normalcy" by the time we reached New York.

Eleanor and the big boys [James and Elliott] are coming down for dinner so I reckon I better take Nan from her carpentening [sic] and think of food.

Take a good swim for me, give my love to "Missy" and come back soon. I miss you lots.

Lovingly, Marion

The women began depositing money into the house account on 23 March 1925; the first deposits were $20 each from Eleanor and Nan; a year later they had accumulated $15,500, with contributions from the three friends about equal. Franklin felt that the first bid the women had received for the construction was too high, and he succeeded in having it lowered by several thousand dollars. Then, as sometimes now, a woman conducting her own business could expect to be asked for the man of the house when a decision was to be made. Franklin was that man. He gave instructions to the architect and to the contractor and workmen, and he paid the bills with Eleanor's, Marion's, and Nan's money from their joint account. The archives at the Franklin D. Roosevelt Library include a file of receipts, letters, and scraps of paper, much like what any one of us would throw in a drawer during a building project. Impressive in their scope, they reveal that FDR was involved at every step of the construction, keeping handwritten notes of the costs.

Franklin found overseeing the cottage a welcome distraction, and he was faithful for a man whose ability to summon enough will to get out of bed was sometimes lacking. A handwritten document ("Bills paid by FDR") shows that the first bill he paid on 25 July was for "hauling stones, $166" and "foundations $222.30." Letters from providers sometimes remind Mr. Roosevelt "again" that their funds are short and he really needs to pay his bills; a few are quite insistent. Marion and Nan are frequently referenced about building matters, Eleanor less so. Franklin did a good deal of business with the local bank and construction firms in Poughkeepsie, as well as ordering special items from places in New York and New Jersey. Eleanor and Nan took particular pride in the fact that local workmen were employed for most of the construction jobs. All of them—Franklin, Eleanor, Marion, and Nan—sometimes together, often at different times, were eager to see the progress made after their absences.

When the costs were added up—about $10,000 for the cottage, $1,939 for the furnishings, and $3,350 for outside work—receipts and disbursements were almost exactly the same among Eleanor, Marion, and Nan. Franklin and Eleanor often accused each other of knowing nothing about finance (public or private), so perhaps this was the first time that together they balanced the books.

Franklin left landscaping the two or three acres to the women, except for protecting trees (and there were almost no substantial trees on the building site). Nan knew they wanted to keep the natural look and in time to add gardens. She began to think about flowerbeds and patios, but she could not begin to do the actual work until the construction phase was over. She assumed the major cost of "out-side improvements": Eleanor and Marion put about $500 each into that account; Nan, more than $8,000. Over the next years she ordered seeds and plants, often from Henderson & Company, noted horticulturalists with a large catalog business and offices in New Jersey and New York City, and began to plant gardens.

Eleanor and Marion likewise recognized Nan's expertise when it came to furnishing the cottage, and they wanted her to design things for their home in a small furniture workshop onsite, which first appeared on architectural plans as a room inside the house (a subject explored in the next chapter). They ordered appliances—a Chambers gas stove and an electric ice box. For upholstered furniture they bought a sofa and chairs from John Wanamaker & Company in New York. The linens came from Macy's and from Lord & Taylor and likely were selected when the women were together in the city. Building and furnishing a house is always a time of stressful exhilaration, not a time for quiet contemplation. But there were times as the cottage rose through the mist off the pond when the three friends must have privately experienced a dream of the house's future and of beauty and modesty and having simple meals by the fire.

The cottage plans called for a main building and a northeast ell that was to be the small workshop for Nan. Each section had a gabled roof. The plans for the inside seem to reflect the women's shared interests. This was a place that related to its setting: a large screened porch across the front looked toward the pond and the bridge over which guests would be seen and heard arriving when the cottage was finished. The spacious two-story main room served as a living and dining room. It was defined by the high ceiling and handsome oak floors. (Franklin estimated that if Nan used some of his big oak trees, it would cost her $12 per square foot; it is not clear whether she agreed to the purchase.) The room had impressive wooden beams in the vaulted ceilings and a handsome flagstone fireplace at the south end where three friends could sit by the hearth, and a corner for Eleanor's desk. Off the main room were a kitchen and a pantry, a novelty for Eleanor, who was not permitted in Sara's kitchen (and perhaps had never asked to be there). Eleanor's one culinary accomplishment was scrambling eggs in a chafing dish for the family on Sunday night in the townhouse after the cooks had gone. Nan liked to cook, though, and she designed the kitchen with open counter spaces and cabinets.

From the living and dining room the women could enter a smaller room that had originally been intended for Nan's workshop until it became clear that she would need more space to build large furniture. It then became a studio with an inglenook where the friends could sit by the fire. It was an intimate space, sheltered from the front of the house, tucked in. On the front next to the main room was a guest room sharing the chimney with the studio, and a bath. Up a flight of stairs with a small landing was a large dormitory-like room with a bath. The floor plan would be changed over the years, but in 1926 Eleanor, Marion, and Nan delighted in sleeping in the same room dormitory-style as if they were college girls. Come summer, patios and the swimming pool that had been dug out of the pond fed by the creek (and later was improved) would begin to define the cottage as a place for outdoor recreation and would become a focal point for picnics throughout FDR's presidency.

On 1 January 1926, the cottage was not yet ready for full occupancy, but Eleanor, Marion, and Nan invited Franklin, Sara, Brud, John, and one of Franklin's physical therapists to come to dinner to celebrate the near-completion. They sat on nail kegs and ate on boards resting on sawhorses. When the therapist suggested that they all make a seat and carry Franklin to the table, he would have none of it and crawled there on his own.[3] He was able to move himself about with his arms now, particularly outside on the grass, although it was sometimes distressing for others to watch. Several years earlier, when Eleanor had seen his efforts for the first time in the house on East 65th Street, she had burst into tears and run from the room. He perfected his sporting mode on the banks of the Val-Kill.

Lunch proceeded, and afterward Franklin organized games for everyone before the boys ran off to work some more on their fort and one of Franklin's men took him back to the car and to Springwood. Eleanor, Marion, and Nan must have hugged one another, happy together at last. They were stalwart middle-aged women who had lived other lives in other places. Having now decided to try communal living, they wasted no time getting on with their adventure. The engraved stationery made it official:

Val-Kill Cottage
Hyde Park, Dutchess County, New York

Telephone: Poughkeepsie 428

Mrs. Franklin D. Roosevelt, Miss Marion Dickerman,

Miss Nancy Cook

A short time later, Stone Cottage was ready for living. The women put out their monogrammed linens, and friends sent gifts of silver, also engraved with the three initials E M N. (The 1922 edition of Emily Post's book on etiquette recommended five to ten dozen monogrammed small hand towels, perhaps excessive for country living.) Franklin gave them accessories and picnic implements for what he called the "honeymoon cottage," and he referred to Eleanor, Marion, and Nan as the "Three Graces." He had chosen a name from Greek antiquity for women of beauty, mirth, and hospitality to the gods. His inscription in a book he gave Marion called Little Marion's Pilgrimage was open and effusive: "To my little pilgrim, whose progress is always upward and onward, to the things of beauty and the thoughts of love and the like—From her affectionate Uncle Franklin, on the occasion of the opening of the love nest on the Val-Kill."[4]

Eleanor freely conveyed to Franklin her pleasure in the life she shared with Marion and Nan: "I was delighted . . . to say goodbye to Mama and come over here for a quiet evening with Nan. I've written two editorials and three letters and we have had supper and the peace of it is divine, but we have to take the 10:05 down tomorrow."[5]

In the early 1970s, after Eleanor's and Nan's deaths, when Kenneth Davis interviewed Marion Dickerman in her home in New Canaan, Connecticut, she told him about the book, Little Marion's Pilgrimage, and the autographed inscription from FDR. She said that businessman Victor Hammer had later "found [the book] somewhere" and returned it to her. She told Davis about (and apparently showed him) an autographed speech from FDR with the inscription, "another first edition for the library of the Three Graces of the Val-Kill."[6]

In calling the cottage the "love nest" in his affectionate inscription, Franklin indulged himself in literary flourishes—he was "Papa"; Marion, the "little pilgrim"; the women were the "three graces." In appropriating a romantic narrative language, Franklin, a wordsmith when he wanted to be, paid homage to Eleanor, Marion, and Nan. In Greek mythology the three graces are creatures of the male imagination, but over centuries women have appropriated the image for themselves. An example is *The Three Graces: Snapshots of Twentieth-Century Women*, by Michal Raz-Russo, a 2012 catalog of an exhibit organized by the Art Institute of Chicago of snapshots of women posed in various ways as the three graces, some outlandish. In tracing the history of an iconic image of women in the first half of the twentieth century, the curator notes that "their engagement with the camera is playful, sultry, and even provocative." The snapshot Nan Cook made of herself, Eleanor, and Marion on Campobello Island in 1926 fits into that tradition of "self-presentation" (see page 90). Placed among other posed graces of the 1920s, Nan's snapshot becomes part of what Raz-Russo calls "a continuum of female representation." Nan had been making snapshots since she was a teenager in Massena, and by the time she had started using a new camera with a self-timer on their trip to Campobello she was experimenting with subject and composition. She captured the three of them in a daring pose on the deck of the summer house. What look does each convey? Marion is self-contained, composed in her expression; Nan is confident, challenging; Eleanor is wary, suspicious. Perhaps each had determined how she would look at the camera, or perhaps it was a moment of spontaneous reaction. Whatever it is, it makes a statement: here we are.

When Eleanor, Marion, and Nan moved into the cottage together, Eleanor, the only wife and mother in the threesome, had passed her fortieth birthday (she would be forty-two in October), had already celebrated her twentieth wedding anniversary, and was the mother of five. Her oldest child, Anna, was a restless young woman who had not wanted to go to college and would marry soon. James was going from Groton, a residential preparatory school for boys near Boston, to Harvard; still at Groton were Elliott, sixteen, and Franklin, twelve. In another two years John would join his brothers at Groton and Eleanor's nest would be empty.

•

A clear schedule of the weeks and months that followed at the cottage has been impossible to re-create because no records have been archived. Apparently the women kept no engagement books in these early years.[7] It is unlikely that they themselves knew from one day to the next how they might spend their time. They were too busy dealing with practical concerns, such as plumbing, heating, furnishings, leaky boats and a rickety bridge, creatures that barked or howled or hooted at night, trees that fell in summer storms, and animals that wandered up from nearby fields.[8]

The first Christmas at the cottage found the women deciding on the right place in the main room to put up their tree. Together they hosted an annual Christmas party for family, friends, and others who worked on the Roosevelt estate. They also agreed that their birthdays would be their own special celebration days and a time of gift giving, and this practice remained true for the rest of their lives. Eleanor generally did not like to celebrate her own birthday (although October was her favorite month at Val-Kill), but she never wanted to miss a friend's, nor did Marion and Nan ever want to miss hers. Eleanor's birthday was 11 October, Nan's was 26 August (Eleanor and Nan were both born in 1884), and Marion's was 11 April (she was seven years younger). If someone was to be out of town or, in Eleanor's case later on, out of the country, they sent cards and gifts ahead of time.

The three friends had become so inseparable that Eleanor did not want to do anything without the other two. When Marion could not join her and Nan for a weekend, she lamented, "It doesn't seem quite right to be seeing things without you," and when she had to go to join Franklin in Warm Springs, a place she did not like, she wrote to them, "I feel I'd like to go off with you and forget the rest of the world existed."[9]

In the spring of 1926 Franklin's mother reported to him, "Eleanor is so happy over there that she looks well and plump, don't tell her so, it is very becoming, and I hope she will not grow thin."[10] Sara's calling attention to Eleanor's weight might, as she knew, have been an awful reminder of the months when her marriage was in crisis and she had looked haggard and depressed. She had not told anyone what had happened, even Isabella Greenway, although on 11 July 1919, she wrote, "This past year has rather got the better of me it has been so full of all kinds of things that I still have a breathless, hunted feeling."[11]

A note Eleanor wrote Marion in 1926 indicates that she had begun to reveal her deepest feelings to her friends. "I have just a minute and want to send you a line. I hate to think that you've been unhappy, dear; it is new for me to have anyone know when I have 'moods,' much less have it make any real difference & if you'll try not to take them too seriously I'll try not to let myself have them."[12]

Biographers have made a good deal of Eleanor's "Griselda moods," in which she sank into depression and silence, never able to say what was troubling her, driving Franklin away and suffering alone. Her note to Marion indicates that in the first months of sharing the cottage she must have allowed Marion and Nan to see her in her unhappy state, and they were not driven away. Marion clearly had expressed concern. What was troubling Eleanor? If Eleanor did not expect Marion and Nan to help solve her emotional problems, she at least had not concealed them. In the spring of 1926 Eleanor's emotional landscape was still fragile. She was happier, but she was subject to depression, especially when it came to Franklin. But her recovery was well under way, and Marion and Nan had a good deal to do with it.

At the same time that Marion gave Eleanor a sense of being cared for, Eleanor reminded Marion that Nan required looking after also. Eleanor apologized for having caused problems in the New York Democratic Women's office when she had asked Louis Howe to help Nan, who had not welcomed his help. She reminded Marion, "One thing at least this week should prove to you, dear, that Nan needs your protection from the world."[13] Eleanor accepted the difficulties of working in an office with Nan because she felt that Nan was worth it. A visitor seeing Nan for the first time described her as "a most determined person who began by being a paid worker at some Democratic organization and then a sort of political secretary to Franklin and now runs the Val-Kill furniture factory as well as the Roosevelt family."[14]

New York State was a boon to Franklin in his run for governor in 1928, and his victory provided a new lease on life together for Eleanor and Franklin. Eleanor and Nan went to Albany on a cold December Saturday to check out the governor's mansion. Eleanor's distancing herself from Springwood had given her confidence in her own decision making, but Nan was intimately involved. It was Nan, not Mama, who would determine how Franklin's family would now live, and Nan was a master at making a house a home. She helped Eleanor decide how to use and furnish the enormous Victorian house with cupolas and towers that sat like a fortress atop a hill in downtown Albany. Fortunately, the outgoing occupants, Al Smith and his wife, Catherine Anne Dunn Smith, had all the huge fireplaces blazing the day Eleanor and Nan showed up. Nothing could have spelled welcome better for Eleanor, who always loved a good fire. As soon as the Roosevelts moved in, she started arranging for visitors and petitioners to have informal talks with the governor. All commented on what a cozy, homelike atmosphere she had created. In fact, it had been done under Nan's direction, and she and Eleanor had had a lot of fun doing it. But at the end of the week, the legislators went home and the Roosevelts left for Hyde Park, where Franklin relaxed at Springwood and Eleanor's heart leapt at the sight of the cottage in the woods.

•

In 1927, as Eleanor developed her interests at Val-Kill, Franklin purchased an old inn and spring-fed swimming pool in Warm Springs, Georgia. When he realized that he could not develop the property as a successful resort and treatment center, he determined to develop it exclusively for polio patients like himself. He was buoyed by the comforting waters (thought to have healing properties) and by the experience of being among other polio patients, and he laughed and encouraged them and felt completely at home. He built his own cottage and found his own picnic spots in the beautiful pine hills of Georgia. Despite her initial misgivings about the cost and about the backwardness of the South, Eleanor came fully to support his choice, even when his plans included Missy LeHand, now his constant companion. Louis Howe remained in New York to keep the home fires burning for FDR's return to politics. Although Eleanor went down for Thanksgiving and occasionally on other weekends, taking Marion and Nan and other friends with her, Warm Springs did not hold the same appeal for her that it did for Franklin. From 1926 to 1928 FDR was to spend nearly half of his time in Warm Springs.[15]

In 1927 Franklin was forty-five years old, but his age did not seem to be a factor in anything he did, perhaps because he had always seemed youthful, and perhaps also because his strenuous efforts to appear sporting made age irrelevant. He was a man determined to walk. He could not have forgotten the weeks of intimacy he had shared with Eleanor in the summer of 1921 as she tended to his physical needs at Campobello. First they had weathered the marital crisis, and now they were moving beyond his crippling disease, which had affected not just him but the family as well.

While Eleanor was making a new life at Val-Kill, Franklin was making a new life for himself in Warm Springs. Henry Toombs, who designed Stone Cottage, now was put to work designing cottages for Franklin, who loved the pine woods and the modest surroundings and was excited by the healing he felt when he was able to stand in the water of the swimming pool. He had the constant companionship of Missy, his secretary and trusted friend, who was absolutely devoted to his every need and who was loved by all the family. Around Missy and Franklin there was a company of local villagers who loved to swap stories with Mr. Roosevelt, as well as old friends and visitors who came to consult with him about his political plans. It was a happy situation—Eleanor with her friends and interests at Val-Kill, Franklin with his at Warm Springs. The two communicated by letter and phone and occasional visits. They were both separate and together. They chose to do whatever they wanted — and that was quite a positive turn of events for their troubled marriage. Eleanor knew his staff and friends at Warm Springs, and he knew hers at Val-Kill. The lines between New York and Georgia were drawn in pleasant places.

6

THE WAY THEY LIVED

The cottage is beginning to look sweet. — Eleanor Roosevelt

A few months after the New Year's Day celebration in 1926, Eleanor wrote Franklin on Val-Kill Cottage stationery, "The cottage is beginning to look sweet."[1] "With the completion of the cottage," Marion remembered, "it became a real home for the three of us. . . . We all were happy and content and Franklin enjoyed it, too. He was glad that Eleanor had found peace and a sense of home in the house which she had taken part in creating."[2] Not until 1933, however, do we have a photograph of the interior (see page 95). Let's have a look around the main room, fully furnished, with a half-dozen pieces made by Val-Kill master craftsman Frank Salvatore Landolfa.

Unlike Springwood, the cottage does not have a stately entrance; the "front door" and the "back door" are simply matters of convenience—you go in the one nearest you. Nor is there a grand front hall like the one at Springwood. This is a true cottage, a small place, a place for like-minded friends. And when it became too small for the invited guests, they moved outside to the porches, the patios, and the swimming pool.

The main room invites comfort and intimacy at the same time that it offers individual spaces when more privacy is needed: the corner desk, which Nan designed, is Eleanor's, with light streaming in the east window. From the window Eleanor could look out over the swamp, where in autumn loosestrife turned red and gold and brown. The desk is open; some papers are settled in cubbyholes, and others are strewn about on the surface. Above the desk is a shelf, also Nan's design, that holds a dozen or so books. There is a sturdy straight-backed chair at the desk, and a round table. Nearby there is a lounge chair with a head pillow, and on the table there are books, cigarettes, a cigarette holder, and a book of matches (Nan and Marion were smokers; Eleanor smoked on occasion). The desk chair turns toward the lounge chair as if two sometimes talk there; when it is turned back to the desk, Eleanor can work while Nan or Marion reads nearby. A three-cushioned skirted sofa with comfortable back pillows faces the fireplace. Someone has left her book on the arm of the sofa. Perhaps on the back of the sofa are Eleanor's or Marion's papers for a class at Todhunter. There is what seems to be another upholstered chair on the right. Except for the straight-backed leather chair against the front wall, behind Nancy's lounge chair, there are no more places to sit. At most, the room seats six or seven people—perhaps Eleanor, Nan, Marion, Caroline O'Day, and let's add Rose Schneiderman and Maud Swartz, two friends who have brought Eleanor into women's union work and who as union workers were less likely to be welcomed by Sara in the Big House.

Another frequent guest was Molly Goodwin, a physical education teacher at the Todhunter School. Marion and Nan had met Molly in England, and she was often an overnight visitor. With the outbreak of World War II she had returned home and enlisted in the Royal Navy; she was sent to the Outer Hebrides, where she charted vessels. After the war she lived comfortably in Sussex, where Marion visited her several times. Some later drawings of Val-Kill show "Molly's room" over the garage.

The round gate-leg table, another of Nan's designs, holds a small brass lamp and a leggy houseplant. Casually scattered across the surface are a seed catalog and various magazines. It is both a place to put out things to be read and a place to drop things off as you come into the room—before you build a fire or turn on the electric tin wall sconces and the lamps.

The overhead chandelier in the main room is a handsome feature. The fire has been laid, the copper kettle for wood is full, and logs are stacked on a grate with circular bronze andirons. Behind the copper kettle fire tools hang from the stone. A hearth brush leans against the fireplace to the left. On the wall above there is a large Navajo rug, possibly a gift from Eleanor's friend in New Mexico, Isabella Greenway, or something Eleanor bought when she was visiting Isabella. The floor rug near the table may also be southwestern. The naval print was a gift from Franklin, whose vast collection still hangs in the entrance hall at Springwood. On either side of the fireplace are two small framed landscape paintings. This is a room for sitting by the fire, for working alone but near others, for reading, and for conversation.

Eleanor's mention in letters and columns of the "sheltered feeling" of sitting by an open fire leads us to imagine her often in this room. There would be a teapot and cups set up on the round table, or perhaps on a small table in front of the fire, where sometimes the women had their simple meals, either prepared by Nan or left by a woman who came from the village to help in the house or kitchen. Unlike Eleanor, Marion and Nan were not used to servants. In the early years before the women held large picnics, it is likely that they made their own meals when they were in residence. When Sara and Franklin and the children were at the Big House, the women were sometimes invited to take their meals there. Sometimes Eleanor, Marion, and Nan had the boys over to spend the night in the cottage, when they likely cooked out.

From the very beginning, family and friends were invited to the cottage to stay in the downstairs guest room. Val-Kill was on occasion a "honeymoon cottage" for guests. The women lent it to Eleanor's daughter Anna and her first husband, Curtis Dall, soon after they married in 1926, and later Eleanor had Nan get the cottage ready for Earl Miller and his new wife. Earl, a New York State trooper, had become one of Eleanor's closest friends after he had been assigned as her bodyguard when Franklin was elected governor of New York in 1928; they traveled together all over the state, gathering information about government affairs in towns and cities, at the same time enjoying each other's company. Although Earl's presence at the Roosevelt dinner table alarmed Mama, he had become a permanent member of the inner circle, loyal to Franklin and especially devoted to Franklin's wife. He felt free to bring his various girlfriends to Val-Kill, and Eleanor accommodated them. Marion and Nan did not like Earl and were alarmed at Eleanor's show of familiarity—Eleanor's hand on Earl's knee—but they knew better than to say so. Earl belonged to the inner circle; best not to tamper with that least they endanger their own special places.

Marion's memories make it possible to re-create one unforgettable evening with Eleanor at Val-Kill. "We were very, very close at that time," Marion said, "and she talked extremely freely."[3] Knowing Marion's words and the setting, we imagine the scene: Soon after they moved into Stone Cottage, in the winter of 1926, Eleanor, Marion, and Nan were sitting by the recessed fireplace in the tucked-away inner sanctum, and Eleanor confided one of her deepest secrets—her discovery of Lucy Mercer's letters to Franklin. Marion remembered, "I never saw [Lucy Mercer Rutherfurd], never heard Franklin mention her, needless to say, I never heard Granny [Franklin's mother]. . . . This was very early in our relationship when Mrs. Rutherfurd was still alive. We never referred to it—she told the story, we were conscious of the depth to which she had been hurt."[4] The closeness of the three women on this occasion seemed to fulfill Franklin's description of them—the three graces who brought joy and a sense of well-being to one another. A great burden must have felt lifted from Eleanor's shoulders when the truth was finally shared. One historian speculates that Eleanor made Marion and Nan promise that they would not choose sides.[5]

The fire had died out, and the glow of embers was fading. They had been sitting for a long time, and still no one had moved. Marion got up and took their trays, but Nan kept her eyes on Eleanor. Finally, Eleanor spoke, so quietly that Marion had to turn to catch her words.

"The bottom dropped out of my own particular world," she said.[6]

The silence deepened.

The next morning a workman bringing a stack of wood let himself in and began stacking it at the hearth. He heard someone speak, and he looked up and saw Mrs. Roosevelt, sitting in the half-light at her desk, and was embarrassed to have disturbed her. She murmured that it was fine; then she gathered some papers and went out of the room. Upstairs Marion and Nan began to talk, but one hushed the other.

Marion and Nan finished dressing and looked at each other. Marion tousled Nan's hair,[7] Nan leaned against her, and they came down the stairs to an empty room.

•

On another night, by Marion's account, the cottage provided sanctuary for Eleanor and Franklin. One summer evening, distraught, Eleanor came to the cottage. She and Franklin had had a "misunderstanding." Marion had known about other misunderstandings, but this one was serious. "She remained closeted with us for three days." Finally, Nan called Franklin at the Big House.

"If you are wise you will come over here," she said, "and right away!"

"But will she talk to me?" he asked.

"You come!"

And so he drove himself to the cottage and sat waiting in the car.

Marion believed that Franklin's "utter helplessness" to get out must have "pierced at last the wall of hurt hostility she had raised against him." Eleanor went out to the car and sat with Franklin for a long time, "more than two hours," and then "she went back to the Big House, and the quarrel was not mentioned again."[8]

Nothing has been uncovered to date this anecdote or suggest what the quarrel was about. It could have been something Mama had said, or it could have been Franklin's usual refusal to hear what Mama had said. Or perhaps Eleanor had refused to spend the night at Springwood. And isn't it possible that, if Eleanor fled to the cottage for whatever reasons and stayed there three nights, this was not the first or the last time? Given the availability of such a safe haven, wouldn't that have been natural?

Sara couldn't understand why Eleanor ever went to the cottage at all. She privately wrote to her own friends to ask their opinion: what is she up to over there? Perhaps Eleanor went to swim in the pool. That explanation did not satisfy Sara; she wanted Eleanor home at Springwood. Alice Roosevelt Longworth, Eleanor's sharp-tongued cousin, relished reporting that someone had heard pillow fights coming from a room in a lodging where Eleanor was staying with friends. Eleanor, it seemed, was frolicking like a girl.[9]

Eleanor was not the only one asked not to sleep away from the Big House. Sara was unhappy when Franklin wanted to build a cottage for himself near Eleanor's, and she insisted that he was never to spend a night there but always return to Springwood. Just as Franklin had overseen the building of their cottage when Eleanor, Marion, and Nan were away, years later Eleanor watched Franklin's cottage going up, cabling him in the summer of 1938, when he was enjoying a restful Pacific cruise, that everything was going well on the construction. Apparently, Franklin never did spend the night at what would be called Top Cottage, but one wishes otherwise, because he had so few remaining years left. He and Daisy Suckley had planned the cottage on what they called their "favorite hill."[10] Soon after he had returned to Springwood to try to rest and recover from the effects of polio, Sara had called Daisy, an unmarried cousin living in her family's Victorian mansion in Rhinebeck on the Hudson, to please come spend time with him. Franklin and Daisy remained the closest of friends, especially in the last years of his life. Private friends were good for Eleanor—and good for Franklin, too.

The unconventional three-way household of Eleanor, a married mother of five, and Marion and Nan, life partners, was boldly conceived, and the fact that friends sent gifts of china and silver showed how they embraced the women's choice to be a family. FDR was being playful in calling the cottage the "honeymoon cottage" and their "love nest," and they felt no need to defend themselves. Franklin didn't have to explain Missy, and Eleanor didn't have to explain Marion and Nan. She did not even feel that she had to explain her choices to her own family. She had changed a great deal from the uncertain little girl she once had been. Once she figured out what she wanted in life, Eleanor had an amazing ability to go her own way.

•

Val-Kill was a testing ground for the forceful woman Eleanor would become. With her share in the cottage and two friends of extraordinary emotional intensity, she had become a nonconforming wife, mother, and daughter-in-law. As she became more independent in her personal life, she became more independent politically. By the end of her life she had moved away from the views of her own class to become a public advocate for women, blacks, Jews, unions, peace, and justice. And in Marion and Nan, who had already defined themselves as progressives, she found two independent spirits and accomplices. Being part of the Roosevelt family elevated them to a new status. Eleanor did not reject all aspects of her privileged life, and she used it to advance her own causes and those of friends, many of them all too willing to ask for favors. The children went to prestigious private schools (Eleanor may have wanted Elliott to try a public school, but she failed to get Franklin's support); she insisted that Anna make her debut; and she lived at good addresses, traveled abroad, drove nice cars, employed a staff, and had her own inheritance and could spend the money she made as she wished. On the other hand, her friends were drawn from different social classes. Mama didn't like the way they looked (so mannish!) or behaved (so casual!) or their uncertain origins (children of immigrants!), but Eleanor welcomed them all to the cottage. Val-Kill was her sanctuary—a safe haven where she could enlarge her intimate circle and her mind.

7

VAL-KILL AS REFUGE

Give us grace. — Book of Common Prayer

If Eleanor, Marion, and Nan wanted Val-Kill to be a refuge from other problems we know nothing about, they expressed their hopes in private conversations we can never recover. The landscape of Val-Kill, however, is a living revelation of nature's gifts: quiet, peace, and beauty. It is a place for solitude as well as for company. Solitude was especially precious for Eleanor, with her large, demanding family and many commitments. She liked to take walks alone, when she could think through what was troubling her. This need to be alone does not contradict all the evidence that she also liked to be around other people. She was still something of a shy introvert, and perhaps remained so all her life despite her strenuous efforts to meet people everywhere.[1]

This is how she might have spent a morning alone:[2] Eleanor had returned to Val-Kill on a November weekend when no one was at the Big House to insist that she stay there, and she had given herself time to do what she wanted. It wasn't easy for Eleanor to be free from responsibility; it was easy for her to do her duty. But she had planned carefully: it was the end of her favorite season, autumn—leaves on the ground, bare branches, winter coming, the morning sun just rising. She stepped outside and breathed in the cold air. She had spent the night in the cottage with Marion and Nan, who were so happy to have her to themselves. And because they had stayed up late talking, Marion and Nan were still sleeping when Eleanor started the car and eased across the bridge for the five-mile drive that would take her to the cemetery at St. James Episcopal Church, where her infant son was buried.

Eleanor sometimes spoke to others about the uncertainties of life—a mother's death, a father's death—but of her own child's death she seems seldom to have spoken except in a few letters to her friend Isabella and on occasion when she was consoling others who had lost a child. She felt that Franklin had never been fully attentive to the grief that had overwhelmed her then. And because she could not talk about it, she withheld a part of herself that no one would ever know.

But this morning she was thinking of the boy she had lost, the first Franklin Jr., born 1 November 1909, who never had a chance to grow up, who died when he was not yet one, twenty years ago. Perhaps her husband remembered, but they had not spoken of it. They seemed unable to communicate their deepest feelings to one another, and each had so little time to talk now that he was governor and she was always on the go.

This was her time; this was her place. As she approached St. James Church, she sensed the presence of the great Vanderbilt estate across the road. She did not turn to look, as passersby often did. She parked in front of St. James, got out, and took a deep breath. Then she slowly stepped through the open gate and into the cemetery and walked to her son's burial place. Kneeling, she laid a few leaves on his stone, speaking words from the Book of Common Prayer: "O God, whose most dear Son did take little children into his arms and bless them; Give us grace, we beseech thee, to entrust the soul of this child to thy never-failing care and love." She stood up and walked away; then, turning back, she moved toward the church. Trying the door and finding it unlocked, she stepped inside.

The church was dark, the early light barely illuminating the stained-glass windows, and without pausing she felt her way hand over hand to the front, where she slipped into the family pew where she had sat so often, and knelt again. When she was finished with her prayers, she left the church as quietly as she had come.

As she crossed the Val-Kill bridge on her return, she paused to look at the cottage, appreciating the way it had made a place for itself in the landscape. The pond reflected the season's changes; already the birds were fewer, the last skeins of migrating geese were long gone to the south, and no frogs jumped into the water to mark her passage. When she entered the cottage, Nan had the teakettle whistling in the kitchen and Marion was making the fire, but both stopped what they were doing and came quickly toward Eleanor. She was home and they had so much time! What would they do? They had their breakfast in front of the fire. Eleanor picked up last night's book and read her favorite parts from Stephen Vincent Benet's *John Brown's Body*, remembering the Shenandoah Valley and a farmer's fields. And for a long time they sat by the fire, until Marion first, and then Nan, stood up and came over and put their hands on Eleanor's shoulders. She reached back and patted them both, and they let the silence come to them.

In the quiet beauty of nature on Campobello Island Eleanor had acquired a sense of peace that she rarely found anywhere else. Now she felt it again in the special magic on the Val-Kill, where woods, creeks, and ponds were the central characters in a play of seasons: in winter, the cottage nestled in deep snow; in spring, bird songs awakened sleepers; in summer, swimmers and sunbathers refreshed themselves; and in the fall, Marion and Eleanor rode horseback or walked the deeper, higher trails.

•

The natural landscape was the perfect setting for Stone Cottage, but Nan saw possibilities to improve it. Perhaps there was nothing that personally satisfied Nan more than gardening. She could do it alone and had no one to please except herself. Soon after the construction site had been stabilized, she began planting, trusting the natural landscape to imprint itself upon her imagination. The heavy work of putting in roads and a driveway and improving the rickety bridge was left to William Plog, the estate superintendent, and the construction crew, and efforts were under way by 1926 to dig out Fall-Kill Creek, recirculating water for a small swimming pool (later closed when a pool better suited to Franklin's needs was built up the hill).

Gardening teaches patience; Nan needed to learn patience. She had an artistic bent, and a garden in many ways reflects the dream life of the gardener. She had unusual energy and skills. Until she designed and planted gardens at Val-Kill, she may not have known herself how talented she was. With the eye of a photographer, she had been studying the landscape for several years; she was now ready to make it hers. Sara Roosevelt had a rose garden and a staff to tend it. Nan was starting out on her own. Eleanor confessed that her own garden experiences were limited to raising radishes in her childhood garden at Tivoli, and Marion preferred active sports—she liked sailing, ice skating, and boating—and left the gardening to Nan. At the end of the day, though, both women were delighted to view Nan's progress.

Like most gardeners, Nan probably spent winter evenings looking at seed catalogs and at magazines like *Better Homes and Gardens* and *House Beautiful* (it was the golden age for women's magazines), but she probably learned best how to garden by doing it. In the first years, Nan, still feeling her way, did not put in many formal gardens. The dense wetland vegetation sheltered the cottage and gave it a feeling of privacy and seclusion, and birch and cedar trees grew along the banks of Fall-Kill Creek. Across the road from Val-Kill was a working farm where FDR's tenant and friend, Moses Smith, raised livestock and crops.

The natural landscape was dramatically different from New York City streets, and the women loved it. The country was quiet; it was a retreat, and it was theirs. But it was not a fortress holding the world at a distance. Nan's was not a secret garden behind high walls and a locked gate. From the very beginning she allowed the way they lived to dictate the terms of her design, placing the formal beds close to the cottage and the patios for outdoor living and allowing the hills, trails, and meadows to invite silences. In time, Eleanor would write in her 26 December 1946 "My Day" column about "the serenity and beauty of a countryside in winter" with a lyricism unexpected from her workaday political prose. "The murmur of the brook under the ice in winter, the little animal marks on the new and untouched snowfall—all of these things are joys which only the country can give us."

8

A GIFT FOR FRIENDSHIP

I think perhaps I would prefer when I am dead to have it said that I had a gift for friendship. —Eleanor Roosevelt

After Eleanor, Marion, and Nan settled in Stone Cottage, their special times were evenings when they could share a simple meal in front of the fire and talk long into the night. At first they were able to sustain the illusion that theirs was a private, exclusive time and place, and the friendship was free and easy. But soon they also had other ideas for themselves—projects they could discuss all the time (organizing statewide Democratic women, a furniture factory, a school in New York)—and the beginnings were stimulating, giving them so much to talk about. After FDR's election in 1928 as governor of New York and his ascension toward the White House, however, Eleanor's interests became so far-reaching and her new friendships so numerous that long before she left Val-Kill for the White House her calendar had begun to fill up with new engagements. Marion and Nan had wanted to be part of Eleanor's life, and they could not have anticipated how often they would not be the magical threesome. Eleanor loved people: once she had become part of the New York network of progressive women, she moved beyond the lonely years when she was a frightened mother and a neglected wife and had no one to talk to. Friends became her family. Ironically, the home life Marion and Nan modeled for Eleanor allowed her to grow well beyond the confines of Val-Kill.

Eleanor Roosevelt understood and embraced her need for friends. "I think perhaps I would prefer when I am dead to have it said that I had a gift for friendship," she said when she spoke about Miss Laura Johnson Wylie, a beloved professor of English at Vassar College for almost four decades, in a service of remembrance in 1934. "I might not see her for weeks," Eleanor said, "but if I went into her house and heard her voice and sat down and talked to her even for a few minutes, I came away with a warm feeling around my heart because she made us conscious of the warmth of her feeling for her friends.... You never went in to see her and came out without feeling a sense of stimulation and refreshment."[1] Eleanor's remembrance of Miss Wylie would be echoed in the remembrances of those who met Eleanor. Martha Gellhorn said about her, "There has never been a woman in public life of the quality, of the nobility, of the pure splendor of Mrs. Roosevelt."[2] Cissy Patterson, a journalist and later owner and publisher of the Washington Times-Herald, believed that Eleanor Roosevelt had accommodated to life better than any woman she had ever known. She said, "I adore her above all women."[3] This kind of affection was based not as much on Mrs. Roosevelt's public service, though it was widely admired by progressives, as on her remarkable personal charisma. In 1922 when Nan chose her as her speaker for a Democratic fund-raiser, she must have sensed immediately from Eleanor's reception in a room full of women that, although she had chosen her for the Roosevelt name, Eleanor left them with "the warmth of her feeling."

•

In the early 1920s one of Eleanor's earliest circles of friends outside New York City was centered in Ithaca, where she made friends with the women who founded Cornell University's program in home economics. She first met Martha Van Rensselaer there in her work with the League of Women Voters, and when Martha and her friend and cohort, Flora Rose, were working to establish a publicly funded school of home economics at Cornell, they often went to talk with Governor Roosevelt about their needs.[4] Eleanor invited them to stay at the governor's mansion on those occasions; at other times they were invited for meetings at Hyde Park. Martha was so interested in the furniture that Nan was making in the shop at Val-Kill that she ordered a Val-Kill partner's desk for her and Flora so that they could work across from one another. Martha and Flora were so inseparable, in fact, that some people called them Miss Van Rose collectively. Scholars of the home economics movement have pointed out that domestic partnerships such as theirs set an example of how fulfilling a female household can be. Their partnership showed that "the proper management of domestic matters both within and outside the home could bring about a more perfect society."[5] Watching Martha and Flora work together reinforced Eleanor's preference for the shared interests of friends.

Eleanor began taking Nan, perhaps the "homemaker" of Val-Kill, with her to Ithaca, and they drove in all kinds of weather to attend the annual Farm and Home Week with thousands of farm women. Eleanor herself was a frequent lecturer at the event, and she liked sleeping in the room where there were photographs of Miss Van Rensselaer, where, even after Martha's death in 1932, her spirit seemed immortal. Also driving with Eleanor and Nan was Elinor Morgenthau, whose husband, Henry, who would become FDR's secretary of the treasury, had studied in the university's agriculture program. Like Eleanor, Martha and Flora had a constant flow of guests, and dinner-table talk always included conversations about the development of statewide programs for women in rural New York and invariably turned into lively planning sessions for upcoming events.

Martha and Flora were not only colleagues; they were a couple, unhappy when they had to be separated. When Martha had a six-month sabbatical in 1931, she wrote Eleanor that she hoped to see her when she came to Washington to help with the White House Conference on Child Health and Protection. However, she explained, "I have so little enthusiasm in regard to my going that I am not burning any bridges behind me." After her signature, "Very affectionately, Martha Van Rensselaer," she added a handwritten note, "Flora is no happier than I am about it."[6] Eleanor wrote similar notes about not wanting to be away from Marion and Nan. She understood Martha's and Flora's dependence on each other and recognized how much work they accomplished together.

Ironically, Eleanor had seldom had a chance to be a "housewife," and the opportunity to learn some domestic skills was exciting. She was impressed by the economy of rural housewives as taught in extension courses offered by Cornell. Many of the tips for economizing that Eleanor applied in the New York governor's mansion and in the White House came straight out of Flora Rose's programs for rural women held at Cornell. She, Elinor, and Nan were frequent participants. Nan had more to learn about how to cook and how to set up their own cottage kitchen, a popular subject for the extension movement. After Eleanor moved into the White House, she tried to have her kitchen prepare some of Flora Rose's seven-and-a-half-cent meals, one of which included hot stuffed eggs, potatoes, bread, prune pudding, and coffee. They proved to be so unpopular with guests and were so ridiculed in the press, however, that she asked her housekeeper, Henrietta Nesbitt, to come up with some new menus. Nesbitt, with no training except in her own kitchen in Dutchess County, was confident that she knew what people liked (simple foods), but despite complaints from many who ate at the White House (including FDR), Eleanor kept Nesbitt for all twelve years. She agreed that perhaps the cheap meals should be served only to the family, not to guests, but she was eager to apply the economic lessons she had learned from the programs at Cornell, and certainly the Great Depression gave her all the reason she needed to save money. She intended to demonstrate that the White House kitchen could serve as a model for "a struggling populace."[7]

For more than thirteen years Eleanor, often accompanied by Elinor Morgenthau, had lectured at Cornell's annual Farm and Home Week to about two thousand women. She kept her promise and came back a few weeks after she had moved into the White House, bringing with her woven goods from Val-Kill looms. The exhibit of Val-Kill goods was intended to show homemakers how they could add to the family income by using skills they acquired through extension courses to make crafts for sale. Nan ran the shop, and Eleanor marketed the goods.

In 1931 after breaking ground for the home economics building at Cornell (which after her death the next year would be named in Van Rensselaer's honor), Martha gave Eleanor credit for having helped make the case to Governor Roosevelt. In time the Martha Van Rensselaer School of Home Economics became the national leader in the field. Behind it was a partnership of women as effective in their work together as in their separate lives. There was no difference between their public and their private spheres. Carrie Chapman Catt, however, took exception to the way Martha and Flora combined work and socializing. "I was interested in the meeting around your breakfast table," she wrote, but she wondered if it was not an "additional burden to the participants."[8]

Another couple who remained among Eleanor's closest friends were like Martha and Flora in that they did not want to be apart and yet had separate interests. Mary ("Molly") Dewson, who called Polly Porter "partner" for all of their fifty-two years together, was a leader of Democratic women, working for FDR's gubernatorial career and later as the head of the Women's Division of the Democratic National Committee. Both Eleanor and FDR turned to her for leadership in pressing the need for New Deal policies. Moss Acre, their summer home in Castine, Maine, was where Eleanor, Marion, Nan, and the children stopped en route to Campobello Island. Perhaps hoping for confirmation that they had made a good decision about Val-Kill, Eleanor, Marion, and Nan need have looked no further for evidence of a felicitous and successful female household than Molly and Polly's commodious house in the woods on Penobscot Bay with rooms for guests. After years of living in a small Greenwich Village apartment in New York City during Molly's political assignments (and Polly's unhappiness) and spending only summers at Moss Acre, in 1952 Molly and Polly retired to live there full time. Although they had lived near Marion and Nan in Greenwich Village, they were not especially close friends. Polly did not participate in their political meetings; she was more interested in her homes, her dogs, and gardens. Molly, a Wellesley graduate, and Polly, a daughter of great wealth, were from a social class different from Marion and Nan, and perhaps Marion and Nan, who had to work for a living, felt this difference keenly. After Molly was out of politics and had moved to Maine, she missed her weekly lunches with Eleanor and felt a little left out.[9] On occasions when Eleanor visited other friends in Castine, Molly was invited to be with them, but Polly stayed home.

Molly and Polly were in a partnership that was extremely close on the domestic level, but Molly's political career was widely divergent from Polly's interests. Eleanor saw that this difference worked well, but perhaps she was as not as sensitive to their division of duties—it was simple for Polly to leave politics to Molly and for Molly to leave the garden and housekeeping to Polly: there was no competition. Friends never seemed to have observed the slightest jealousy between the two. In fact, Polly was known to tell friends who might have wondered if she was as "smart" as Molly that Molly had chosen her.

Molly, like Eleanor a consummate New Yorker, once gave up a political appointment that would have required her to work in Washington because Polly was unhappy when Molly was away politicking. In Maine, Molly kept up her political interests (she even ran for a local office, and lost) and a correspondence with old friends. Polly kept dogs and gardens. Together they often entertained and were entertained. At night, Polly read aloud as Molly did the mending by the fire. They made scrapbooks and diaries of their long lives together, documenting their travels, their efforts to farm, birthdays, books they read aloud, letters written and received, occasions with family and friends, and daily observations about the weather.[10]

For having worked for FDR's 1932 election Molly was honored at a special dinner and presented with a gift—a chest of drawers from Val-Kill Industries (the subject of a later chapter). Later, after the Democratic Convention in July 1936, Eleanor invited a group of women that included Molly, Caroline O'Day, and Frances Perkins to Val-Kill for a weekend of relaxation and planning. Eleanor asked Nan to be the hostess. She could always count on Nan to get things ready, and the food and camaraderie were good. After they worked together, Molly wrote to Eleanor, "You are sort of my Mother Earth that I need to touch once in a while."[11]

•

Perhaps the longest-lasting and most amicable friendship with a female couple, and the one that most deserves to be compared to Eleanor's friendship with Marion and Nan, was her friendship with Esther Lape and Elizabeth Read, described earlier as part of a New York City women's network. They had met in 1920 in New York, and Eleanor continued her friendship with Esther after Elizabeth's death in 1943 — in late summer of 1962 coming home from Campobello, Eleanor made her last trip to Salt Meadow, their Westport, Connecticut, country home, only months before her death. There is no evidence that they ever quarreled. In fact, Eleanor looked to Esther and Elizabeth as a calming presence and often sought their wise advice as they worked together for world peace against the vocal opposition of political opponents. Eleanor and her secretary Malvina "Tommy" Thompson often took stacks of mail to be answered in the quiet woods of Salt Meadow. Beyond discussing their political interests, however, Eleanor often turned to Esther and Elizabeth to discuss personal things that were troubling her.[12] Eleanor's closeness to Esther and Elizabeth was reinforced by Tommy's confidence in them. Although Tommy eyed all of Eleanor's friends with some suspicion that they were using her, she seems never to have questioned Esther's and Elizabeth's motives. Tommy simply thought that they were the best friends Eleanor could have, and they were her friends, too.

Esther, a graduate of Wellesley, had taught English at Swarthmore College and at Barnard College and was a progressive activist for world peace and health care. She expressed effortlessly a kind of "class" — she moved with ease among varied groups, from the League of Women Voters to the American Committee on Russian Relations, favoring the recognition of the Soviet Union. Eleanor admired Esther's intellectual brilliance. By the time Eleanor met her in 1920 in the New York State League of Women Voters — Esther was one of the founders — Esther was well known as a journalist and researcher. She was a youthful thirty-nine-year-old: stylish, beautifully dressed, confident, and graceful. She was elegantly partnered to Elizabeth, whom she adored; Elizabeth was a graduate of Smith College, with a master's degree from Columbia University, and a graduate with distinction from the law school of the University of Pennsylvania, and a practicing New York attorney. Elizabeth became Eleanor's attorney and adviser on many things as they studied the *Congressional Record* to keep Eleanor informed. Elizabeth was forty-eight years old, almost a decade older than Esther, and their age difference also expressed how well they related: Esther looked after Elizabeth, and Elizabeth made a happy home—she even felled trees at Salt Meadow, though she was not physically up to the task, but she wanted to perfect their landscape as she did their home.

In 1924 a Washington newspaper photographer captured Eleanor and Esther on their way to a Senate hearing about the Bok Peace Prize, an award that would be given for the best plan for how the United States could contribute to world peace (see page 95). Members of the Senate were aroused in opposition to this prize, and Esther and Eleanor came under considerable fire. When the Senate turned it down, they kept their cool and continued working for the World Court. The photograph tells a story of two handsomely dressed women striding with confidence into a Senate hearing: the man in the background may be a newspaperman who thinks he recognizes Mrs. Roosevelt, or perhaps he is impressed by the women's fashion in an environment of business suits. In January 1924 Eleanor was certainly recognizable, and Esther's photo had been in the papers as the administrator of the Bok Prize. More than 22,000 proposals on ways to achieve peace were submitted, and Esther chose 20 of them to publish with her own analysis. The award received even more attention when Esther revealed that Eleanor Roosevelt and Narcissa Vanderlip, a progressive Republican and friend of Eleanor's and Esther's, were on the selection committee. The Senate had investigated charges that the Bok Peace Prize was a tool of "foreign governments or foreign institutions," and eventually the hearings were suspended. There is nothing that bonds friends more closely than to have shared a lost cause, especially one as noble as world peace. Esther and Elizabeth were the most idealistic of all of Eleanor's close friends, and Eleanor used them as a touchstone. They made the news as women going up against powerful U.S. senators, and they were taken seriously. Franklin's friend and supporter Josephus Daniels wrote to tease Franklin about his wife's news-making overshadowing her husband's, relieved that he was not "the only 'squaw' man in the country."[13]

In addition to her work for world peace, Esther took on another large cause: improved health care for all Americans; she used Eleanor to reach FDR to ask for his support. In 1937 she edited a two-volume report, titled American Medicine: Expert Testimony out of Court, from doctors in disagreement with the argument of the American Medical Association that health care was already adequate. Health care remained Esther's lifelong interest well into the 1950s, and Eleanor continued to work with her to advance progress in health and medical research. They served together on the board of the American Foundation, which had published American Medicine.

When they were in New York City, Esther and Elizabeth maintained a beautiful apartment in Greenwich Village where their personal chef served a fine cuisine to their women friends, followed by stimulating literary readings and discussions. This setting reminded Eleanor of her happy years with Mlle Souvestre at Allenswood in England more than any other place she had ever known. Over the door of their house at Salt Meadow Elizabeth had carved Plato's invocation to Pan, the god of the woods and fields, which petitions, "Give me beauty of the inward soul; and may the outward and inward man be one."[14] Their motto, Toujours gai, was painted over the lintel. Eleanor and Tommy, her secretary, often visited Esther and Elizabeth at Salt Meadow, and when Elizabeth was too busy to see them Eleanor and Tommy talked with them by phone. In this case, Eleanor and Tommy and Esther and Elizabeth had struck the perfect balance.

In another respect, Esther and Elizabeth were models for Eleanor: they wore expensive clothes, and they ordered the best fabrics and shopped at the best dressmakers. After Eleanor had met them in 1920, they had begun to influence her wardrobe and sense of style by recommending their own tailors. Eleanor had purchased clothes in Europe—during her honeymoon and when she returned with Franklin in 1919—but she did not spend a lot of time shopping in New York. She clearly had paid careful attention to her clothes on the day she and Esther were photographed on their way to testify before Congress. From hats to shoes, the women are elegantly dressed in black. Eleanor was forty, Esther forty-two (their October birthdays are three days apart). Esther wore a fur piece and a shorter skirt with a stylish kick-pleat, Eleanor had satin cuffs and collar; they matched one another stride for stride, watching their steps.

In some ways, Eleanor's relationship with Esther and Elizabeth was the longest, most continuous, and best of her close friendships. There was never a rift between them for over a half-century. Considering all of Eleanor's friends, Esther and Elizabeth seem from this distance to be the ideal companions. The threesome worked beautifully because they were so harmonious together. The friendship changed somewhat when Elizabeth's health began to fail, and Eleanor shared Esther's deep grief when Elizabeth died in December 1943. Eleanor returned to Salt Meadow to keep company with Esther, and the following spring at Esther's request she planted bulbs where Elizabeth's ashes had been scattered. Eleanor and Esther continued to work together for the rest of Eleanor's life.

A quite different friend to Eleanor was Rose Schneiderman, who directed the New York Women's Trade Union League. She and her lifelong companion, Maud Swartz, who had learned organizing in the British labor movement, taught Eleanor about trade unions. They were stalwart working-class women, unafraid to confront authority in defense of a woman's right to equality. They met in 1922, and Eleanor's authenticity appealed to Rose; the two women became instantly allied in their interests. Marion and Nan were also close friends within the circle of labor activists. Rose, a daughter of religious Jews who had emigrated from Poland, was a dynamic speaker who had galvanized her audience when she spoke after the Triangle Shirtwaist Factory fire in 1911 (Joseph Lash called her a "a redheaded packet of social dynamite").[15] By the time Eleanor met Rose, she was one of the most recognized leaders of the women's trade union movement. When she entertained working women in the clubhouse of the New York Women's Trade Union League, which Eleanor supported, she invited Eleanor to read to them, followed by cookies and hot chocolate, which Eleanor brought. Eleanor in turn invited Rose to the Roosevelt twin house at East 65th Street for a Sunday night supper of scrambled eggs (Eleanor's only accomplishment as a cook, not counting roasting hot dogs at Val-Kill). She felt less free to invite Rose and Maud to Sara's house in Hyde Park, but she sometimes did, and she invited them to Val-Kill and to the summer cottage on Campobello Island, too, where they engaged in lively conversations with Marion and Nan. When Eleanor once left the island briefly to take care of other family matters, she reassured Franklin that she left Rose and Maud in charge of the boys, believing that they were far more capable of handling them than the children's tutor.

Sara did not want her grandchildren exposed to the "riffraff" of the lower neighborhoods that Rose and Maud knew so well, but Eleanor defied her. She got her sons to send out invitations to a Christmas party to children of Trade Union League members. Eleanor bought gifts, Nan decorated the Christmas tree, and the boys, somewhat reluctantly, had their first introduction to families unlike those they had known. Frances Perkins, FDR's secretary of labor, later credited the president's education about trade unions to Eleanor's friendship with Rose and Maud.

Eleanor's and Franklin's enduring friendship with Elinor and Henry Morgenthau Jr. was safely in their social class, both couples being from important New York families. Elinor worked in Eleanor's women's organizations, and Henry became FDR's close friend and adviser—and eventually his secretary of the treasury. He was the son of Henry Morgenthau Sr., Woodrow Wilson's ambassador to Turkey. The Morgenthaus had a beautiful house and a nearby farm in Hopewell Junction in southern Dutchess County, where they raised cattle and apples. Eleanor sometimes spent the night with Elinor when they were setting forth on travels, and she and Franklin attended the Morgenthaus' large cookouts.

Among Eleanor's closest friends, Elinor was exceptional: she was happily married, and her first priority was her own family—she and Henry had three children. Eight years younger than Eleanor, she was the daughter of a woolen manufacturer; her maternal grandfather had been a founding partner in Lehman Brothers. Expressing an early interest in the theater, she was active in the drama society at Vassar College. Eleanor envied Elinor for her college education, and Elinor's affiliation was one of the reasons that Eleanor was drawn to Vassar— that and Vassar's close proximity to Hyde Park, and the fact that it was an outstanding woman's college. Vassar played an important role in Eleanor's and Elinor's lives, keeping them close to young people and to the intellectual and social lives of the college's outstanding women faculty members.

Like Eleanor, Elinor had volunteered in a settlement house, located in Manhattan's Lower East Side, the home of poor Jewish families. Elinor and Henry were Jews, but they cultivated life outside Jewish circles and stayed away from controversy, calling little attention to themselves as Jews. After the Nazis rose to power in Germany, however, they became publicly active in behalf of America's intervention in the war.

Eleanor's close friendship with Elinor helped her come to terms with her early anti-Semitism, recorded in letters between Eleanor and her mother-in-law written after meeting Jews at New York parties. In the 1920s Sara invited Elinor and Henry Morgenthau to a party at Springwood, however, and found them an attractive couple, and she and Eleanor began to soften their views.[16] Thereafter, Henry and Elinor were included at many Roosevelt occasions, on FDR's houseboat in Key West, at Springwood, and in Washington. When Eleanor and Elinor began working for the Democratic Women's Division, they traveled together with Marion, Nan, and Caroline O'Day, organizing women throughout New York State. In 1928 the Morgenthaus were proud to serve as alternate delegates to the Democratic National Convention. Eleanor wrote FDR, "Elinor and Henry are like children in their joy that she should be made a delegate at large—I never realized anyone could care so much."[17]

In later years the Morgenthaus and Eleanor became ardent advocates of the new state of Israel. By then, Eleanor had other close Jewish friends—young Joseph Lash and his wife, Trude Pratt Lash, and David Gurewitsch, her personal doctor, and his wife, Edna. Now that she had a more public voice of her own, she became a powerful advocate for Jews at a time when many of her contemporaries still harbored anti-Semitic views. Eleanor's earlier expressions of anti-Semitism had been harsh, and FDR's willingness to confront what was happening to Jews in Nazi Germany was late in coming, but slowly both of them were moving beyond their own time and place in the midst of a changing world. Elinor Morgenthau, neither a firebrand nor an aggressor, was key to Eleanor's transformation. She was very sensitive to slights and felt that friends like Marion and Nan did not like her because she was a Jew. In 1937 when Eleanor proposed Elinor for membership in the exclusive women's Colony Club in New York City, she was blackballed because she was Jewish. Eleanor then resigned from the club. Elinor was a noble woman, and she deserves more recognition than she has received.

Elinor Morgenthau increasingly had heart problems that restricted what she did, and she died in 1949 when she was only fifty-seven years old. At her memorial service Eleanor spoke of her great admiration for Elinor as a wife and mother. Elinor's choice to put her husband and children at the center of her life had been different from Eleanor's, and Eleanor admired that decision even as she made a different one.

For more than thirty years Eleanor maintained another relationship that may have been more a romance than a friendship, but in the absence of any correspondence that may have been exchanged between them, we cannot be certain. It was different from the earlier friendships I have described because this friend was a man, often single—he married and divorced several times. He was Earl Miller, whom Eleanor first met in 1918 when he was assigned to be FDR's navy escort. But in 1929 when he was assigned to serve as bodyguard to the First Lady in the New York governor's mansion, their friendship blossomed. She was forty-four, and he was thirty-two. It was a dangerous, tantalizing age for both of them; each had had failed marriages. Earl saw something others did not see: a woman who needed the kind of emotional companionship that he needed himself as an orphan, and they began to confide in each other; he could make her laugh, and encouraged her to smile for photographers. He showed respect—he called her "the Lady"—but he did not hesitate to stand close to her or to touch her. Of course, because they spent so much time together, family members and friends wondered whether they were lovers. There is no evidence that they were. Earl had a unique place in Eleanor's life: she was first among his relationships, which may have contributed to his three failed marriages. He protected her against any and all critics and thought that Franklin had been cruel in his faithlessness. No one was going to alter the fact that they had an exclusive loyalty to each other. Earl accompanied her on many trips, and he gave her the horse she loved to ride and the dogs that were also her protectors. He taught her to dive into the Val-Kill pool (never very successfully) and to target shoot. She blossomed under his attentions: he was a young, fit, handsome athlete who liked to show off his body, moving about the swimming pool in his brief bathing suit, preening and prancing, and thus offending Marion and Nan but apparently delighting Eleanor. She was flirtatious with this much younger man whom everyone found handsome. She took time off from her busy schedule to help him move into new apartments, which she cleaned and furnished. Above all, she could count on him to put her first. And he was more circumspect than any of her other intimates; their letters have never been recovered, and he refused to divulge any details about their relationship. His loyalty to her was absolute.[18]

All in all, Eleanor had a crowded dance card. She had always had a great knack for making friends. At Allenswood she had been singled out as the most popular girl in the school, and Mlle. Souvestre wrote to Eleanor's grandmother that Eleanor had the warmest heart of anyone she had ever known. That popularity continued over a lifetime, and she held together many circles of friends. When her close friends eyed one another jealously, she managed to ignore the rivalries and did not hesitate to invite one friend to come in as the previous one left. So what if Marion and Nan didn't like Earl or Esther and Elizabeth, and what if many friends found Elinor difficult? She ignored what she did not want to confront. She had learned that tactic from the master, FDR.

Eleanor had another tactic for managing her relationships: she liked being one of three. This preference perhaps allowed her to be part of but distant from an exclusive relationship with one person. (The threesome of Eleanor, Franklin, and Mama, however, was impossible.) Before setting up housekeeping with Marion and Nan, she had already enjoyed a close friendship with Esther and Elizabeth, spending many evenings in their apartment in Greenwich Village, where Eleanor herself would rent a small "hideaway" during the White House years. Perhaps it was Eleanor's pleasure in the romance of an all-female household that worked so well with Elizabeth and Esther that led her so quickly to build the cottage with Marion and Nan. When they met Eleanor, they had been a couple for more than a decade, so that part of the three-sided triangle was already securely in place. Eleanor was careful not to come between them. As long as she deferred to them, harmony prevailed. As she became more independent, however, she began to require more space for herself.

Fifteen-year-old Eleanor Roosevelt, a student of Allenswood, in the back row, third from right. Courtesy of the Franklin D. Roosevelt Presidential Library and Museum, Hyde Park, N.Y.

Nan Cook and friends play cards at home in Massena, N.Y. Courtesy Bonnie and Gary Cook.

Nan Cook, Marion Dickerman, and Eleanor Roosevelt packed and ready for camping. Courtesy of the Cook-Dickerman Collection, Eleanor Roosevelt National Historic Site, National Park Service.

Peggy Levenson (Marion's sister, who taught French at Todhunter), Nan Cook, Eleanor Roosevelt, and Marion Dickerman during a July 1926 camping trip. Courtesy of the Cook-Dickerman Collection, Eleanor Roosevelt National Historic Site, National Park Service.

Eleanor Roosevelt, Nan Cook, and Marion Dickerman en route to Campobello. Courtesy of the Franklin D. Roosevelt Presidential Library and Museum, Hyde Park, N.Y.

Eleanor Roosevelt, Marion Dickerman, and Nan Cook at the Roosevelts'
summer home, Campobello Island. Courtesy of the Franklin D. Roosevelt
Presidential Library and Museum, Hyde Park, N.Y.

Roosevelt Summer Home, Campobello Island. Courtesy of the Cook-
Dickerman Collection, Eleanor Roosevelt National Historic Site,
National Park Service.

Marion Dickerman, Russell (the Roosevelt boys' tutor), Captain Calder, Franklin Jr., Eleanor Roosevelt, Henry Roosevelt (Eleanor's brother Hall's son), John, and George Draper (the son of Eleanor's doctor) picnic on the beach at Campobello. Courtesy of the Cook-Dickerman Collection, Eleanor Roosevelt National Historic Site, National Park Service.

Franklin Jr., Marion Dickerman, John Roosevelt, and Eleanor Roosevelt on the deck of the *Regina*, headed for Europe, summer 1929. Courtesy of the Cook-Dickerman Collection, Eleanor Roosevelt National Historic Site, National Park Service.

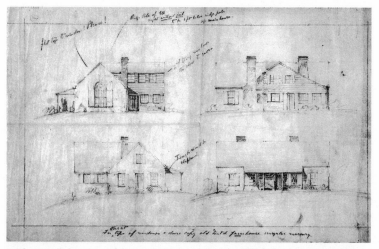

Early pencil drawing of Stone Cottage. Courtesy of the Cook-Dickerman Collection, Eleanor Roosevelt National Historic Site, National Park Service.

Stone Cottage, 1920s to 1930s. Courtesy of the Franklin D. Roosevelt Presidential Library and Museum, Hyde Park, N.Y.

Springwood in the snow, 1920s. Courtesy of the Franklin D. Roosevelt Presidential Library and Museum, Hyde Park, N.Y.

Anna Roosevelt and Eleanor Roosevelt in a Val-Kill snow. Courtesy of the Franklin D. Roosevelt Presidential Library and Museum, Hyde Park, N.Y.

Eleanor Roosevelt, FDR, Missy LeHand, and Earl Miller at the Val-Kill swimming pool. Courtesy of the Franklin D. Roosevelt Presidential Library and Museum, Hyde Park, N.Y.

Nan Cook (seated), Eleanor Roosevelt, Caroline O'Day, and Marion Dickerman work in the office of the New York City Democratic Women. Courtesy of the Cook-Dickerman Collection, Eleanor Roosevelt National Historic Site, National Park Service.

Esther Lape and Eleanor Roosevelt in Washington, D.C., on the way to a congressional hearing for the Bok Peace Prize. Courtesy of the Franklin D. Roosevelt Presidential Library and Museum, Hyde Park, N.Y.

Stone Cottage main room, 1930s, with interior furnishings designed by Nan Cook and produced by Val-Kill Industries. Courtesy of the Cook-Dickerman Collection, Eleanor Roosevelt National Historic Site, National Park Service.

Eleanor Roosevelt and Nan Cook at Nan's drawing board at Val-Kill Industries. Courtesy of the Cook-Dickerman Collection, Eleanor Roosevelt National Historic Site, National Park Service.

Nan Cook and Eleanor Roosevelt with a National Recovery Administration poster at Val-Kill Industries. Courtesy of the Cook-Dickerman Collection, Eleanor Roosevelt National Historic Site, National Park Service.

Nan Cook
finishes
furniture at
Val-Kill Industries.
Courtesy of the
Cook-Dickerman
Collection,
Eleanor Roosevelt
National Historic
Site, National Park
Service.

Eleanor Roosevelt
in class at the
Todhunter School.
Courtesy of the
Cook-Dickerman
Collection, Eleanor
Roosevelt National
Historic Site,
National Park
Service.

Todhunter School students at Val-Kill pond. Courtesy of the Cook-Dickerman Collection, Eleanor Roosevelt National Historic Site, National Park Service.

Marion Dickerman seated on steps near the cottage at Val-Kill. Courtesy of the Cook-Dickerman Collection, Eleanor Roosevelt National Historic Site, National Park Service.

(*opposite*) Eleanor Roosevelt with her first grandchild (Anna's daughter), Ellie (often called "Sistie"), on their way to the Todhunter School. Courtesy of the Cook-Dickerman Collection, Eleanor Roosevelt National Historic Site, National Park Service.

Cuff Links Gang celebrating FDR's birthday on January 30, 1934, with costumes as Emperor Roosevelt and his court. Nancy Cook and Eleanor Roosevelt are to FDR's right, and his daughter Anna is on his other side. Marion Dickerman is to FDR's far left, above Louis Howe in helmet. Courtesy of the Franklin D. Roosevelt Presidential Library and Museum, Hyde Park, N.Y.

Eleanor Roosevelt square dances at the federal homestead in Arthurdale, West Virginia. Courtesy of the Franklin D. Roosevelt Presidential Library and Museum, Hyde Park, N.Y.

Eleanor Roosevelt and Nan Cook with some of FDR's advisers at a Val-Kill picnic. Courtesy of the Franklin D. Roosevelt Presidential Library and Museum, Hyde Park, N.Y.

Marion Dickerman at the wheel with Eric Gugler, sculptor of the UN monument to Eleanor Roosevelt. Courtesy of the Cook-Dickerman Collection, Eleanor Roosevelt National Historic Site, National Park Service.

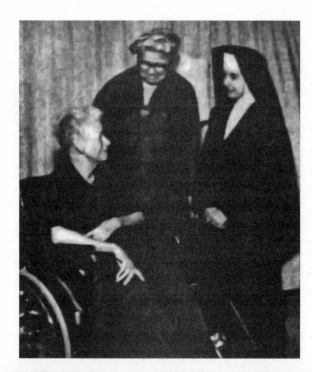

Eleanor Roosevelt visiting Nan Cook at St. Joseph's Manor in 1962 with one of the Carmelite sisters in charge of the nursing home in Trumbull, Connecticut. Courtesy of the *Trumbull Times*.

Eleanor Roosevelt Memorial Bench (1966), United Nations Garden, New York City. Sculpted by Eric Gugler. UN Photo/Lois Conner.

9

IT'S UP TO THE WOMEN

Furnish an example in living. . . . Have a knowledge of life's problems and an imagination. . . . Allow your children to develop along their own lines. . . . Have vision yourself and bigness of soul. —Eleanor Roosevelt

As Eleanor anxiously anticipated moving to the White House after the March 1933 presidential inauguration, she hurried to establish her own identity, editing her father's letters to her (*Hunting Big Game in the Eighties*) and writing *It's Up to the Women*, a primer for getting through hard times. She reached back to the past, and she looked forward to the future, but there was more poignancy than a sense of urgency. Her father's letters affirmed his love for her, and she clung to that love like a lost child. *It's Up to the Women* was a guide to what women could do to help their families, communities, and nation through hard times. Both books were the product of wishful thinking and did not plumb the depths of her subjects. Her father did love her dearly, and she, him, but he abandoned her and died an alcoholic. She observed that women could be good wives and mothers, that they should economize even if they are women of wealth, and that even the average homemaker could find ways to make do and should consider getting a job outside the home—perhaps the most challenging idea in the book. All of these efforts should be done with a "bigness of soul," a phrase she had used in an earlier (unpublished) essay describing "Ethics of Parents." For many women, what she expected of them was a staggering assignment, though couched in the most reasonable way, well beyond the reality of their lives. It hardly reflected her own difficulties. Her view that women had always carried America through hard times was true enough, but for most women, saving their families and their country was an unattainable goal. She was whistling in the dark, while facing daunting prospects in her own life of what lay ahead when she moved to Washington.[1]

"It's up to the women," however, was a colloquial phrase and an apt description of the way she, Marion, and Nan were trying to hold the Roosevelt family together, keep their own projects going, and further FDR's career. It is as apt today as it was then: women really are expected to do it all, and Eleanor's determination to live up to that standard both thrilled and exasperated her friends. How could anyone keep up with Eleanor Roosevelt? Marion and Nan must have asked themselves that question every day. Sometimes their dear friend Eleanor's charge to herself seemed to be, "It's up to me."

During FDR's two terms as governor of New York (1928–32), Eleanor, Marion, and Nan were able to stay closely connected because they were sharing both their own work and FDR's. Eleanor and Marion taught together. Marion and Nan were invited to Albany to attend special events. Eleanor saw them often in New York City and at Hyde Park, where Sara invited them to meals at Springwood, and they invited their own guests to Val-Kill. Each of them engaged individually in many public activities and projects as well. With FDR's political career and the large Roosevelt family's needs added, their lives were a rich brew. Eleanor could have given up her own ambitions and tended to hearth and home, but of course she did not. She had found the ideal life—shared public interests with close personal friends.

Eleanor urged women to work for paid wages out of the home, and she took her own advice. Soon after they built the cottage, she and Marion and Nan started Val-Kill Industries to make reproduction furniture, and they bought a private school (subjects of later chapters). The success Eleanor enjoyed as a teacher at the Todhunter School empowered her as nothing else had. She prepared lessons, she presented complex materials in a way that high school girls could understand, she kept up with current events that she wanted her students to be aware of, she arranged field trips, and she did it all on the run—racing to catch a train for the commute between Albany and New York. She also was paid her first earned income—except for being paid for magazine articles, which became a steady source. Marion's schedule as director and teacher at the school was also demanding, especially given her constant concerns about satisfying parents and recruiting new students for each new year. Back in the shop at Val-Kill Industries, Nan was dealing with craftsmen who had their own ideas about how things should be run.

Another factor played a big role in the women's lives: the five Roosevelt children. Allowing children to develop along their own lines, as Eleanor recommended in It's Up to the Women, wasn't exactly working out for Anna, James, Elliott, Franklin Jr., and John. Eleanor was often emotionally upended as her children chose to marry young and then divorce: the first, Anna, married in 1926 and was divorced in 1934, a pattern the other four children experienced. Eleanor was determined to remain friends with the former spouses of her children. Remembering how she and Franklin had suffered when Sara interfered in their lives, Eleanor tried to stay out of her children's lives. Sara, however, still tried—and failed—to control her grandchildren's lives, especially when it came to their disastrous marriages. The tensions between her and Eleanor resurfaced as each of them failed to discipline the children. Eleanor made more of an effort to ignore Mama, perhaps because she now had her own life. Mama, for her part, remembered Eleanor's heroic role in nursing Franklin at Campobello. She was rarely, if ever, critical of Franklin, and now she was less likely to be critical of Eleanor, especially as it became clear that her son's election as New York governor put him exactly where he wanted to be. Sara did not, however, think that Eleanor was a very good mother because she had failed to teach the children "right from wrong." Eleanor was not sure that her own notions of right and wrong—if she knew them herself—would satisfy her mother-in-law. Bringing up the Roosevelt children was a hit-or-miss affair, and although they went to the best schools (except for Elliott, who refused to go to any college), traveled, drove new cars, and chose new romantic relationships whenever it suited them, there is a case to be made that they were not well parented. The children said so themselves, some in letters, some in publications. FDR himself said it was a terrible thing to be a child of the president of the United States.

Eleanor as a "bad mother" became a popular stereotype led in part by Eleanor's own sense of guilt and, after her death, aided and abetted by her sons in books about their parents. In recent years, however, now that the complexity of women's lives has become better understood, Eleanor Roosevelt is due a reprieve. Fortunately, she had grandchildren who adored her, and that adoration has continued down through the generations. Some who have been interviewed often—Anna's first child, Eleanor "Ellie" or "Sistie" (Seagraves), and her cousin, Nina Roosevelt (Gibson), John and Anne's daughter, remember the guest house in Stone Cottage and Val-Kill as "paradise" and remember Grandmère with respect and affection that surpasses even her public reputation.[2] Periodically, a wedding notice appears in the *New York Times* announcing that a relative of Eleanor and Franklin has married.

When Eleanor, Marion, and Nan moved into the cottage, they could not remove themselves from Eleanor's family. Franklin and the children complicated their lives in ways that they seem not to have considered. Even after the children were adults, Eleanor was still a mother, perhaps with a greater sense of duty to try to make up for what she had felt was her neglect in earlier years. She rushed to their bedsides when they were sick; visited their houses, spread out across the country, to get to know their families; sent them money when they needed it (which they often did); and tried to be available whenever they turned up and to keep their father informed of their latest decisions (he was often unavailable). Despite her disappointments, she accepted their divorces (she encouraged Anna's love affair with John Boettiger, whom Anna later married) and her new daughters-in-law. Increasingly, Anna became closer to her mother, but the boys turned more often to their grandmother, who continued to supply them with cars, money, and houses. (Sara's gift of a house as a wedding present for Anna and Curtis Dall—without telling Eleanor—hurt Eleanor deeply.)

Marion and Nan were aware of the dramas always going on in the Roosevelt family. Looking after young boys on a camping trip, however, had been easy compared with trying to keep up with willful adults. Years earlier, Marion and Nan as partnered women had simplified their lives even as they made a deliberate choice to be a couple without children, a relationship that lasted for a half-century. Eleanor assumed that Marion and Nan could look after each other. Her children could not. So, as Eleanor's and Franklin's public lives became more complicated, Marion and Nan had reason to feel unsettled. They were living close to one of the great unfolding stories of American political life. The future was still uncertain, and how future events would affect them in terms of being able to live normal lives remained to be seen.

Eleanor could never quite persuade herself that she had done enough to help the less fortunate, which is why she seldom had leisure time. She was not reluctant to pick up hitchhikers and bring them home. Eleanor regularly invited troubled New York City boys from the Wiltwyck School across the river. One of them, Claude Brown, grew up to describe in Manchild in the Promised Land (1965) the "lady with the squeaky voice" who welcomed him and his Wiltwyck schoolmates to her picnics. And not only did Eleanor and Franklin have a large family that produced many grandchildren, but there were also the children of Eleanor's friends and of staff members and neighbors. Nan's pictures show the swimming pool full of local children, whose parents kept their own scrapbooks of the occasions. Whether you were the chauffeur or the cook or the gardener, you were part of life at Val-Kill.

Marion especially, and Nan too, loved to invite children of nearby families over to sit on their patio and play with their dog, Dean. They took the children for walks, told them stories, and helped them with their lessons. Marion and Nan were very good "aunts," and when the Roosevelt boys rebelled at having Marion as their tutor, it was not for want of love on Marion's part. Rebellious boys often do not like to be made to do their lessons. Marion and Nan initially knew very little about bringing up children and nothing about Eleanor as a mother.

They learned how to be easy with the two younger boys, gamely keeping up with their adventures. And they tried to follow the adult children's lives and marriages. Eleanor's family was a complicating factor. She expected loyalty to her adult children, no matter how often she herself privately despaired of their behavior. And if Marion and Nan took the children's side in some dispute, Eleanor could bristle with jealousy.

One wonders how much Marion and Nan came to understand about Eleanor and motherhood. Did they praise her for the children's successes or blame her for their failures? How often were they overwhelmed by Eleanor's large family and unsure what their roles in it were supposed to be? The children wandered down on weekends to swim in the pool. Sometimes Brud and John spent the night at the cottage. Once Brud was late for lunch, and Marion waited for him. When he finally got to the cottage, he explained breathlessly that he had just seen a calf born. When he asked if that was the way babies were born, Marion said, "Pretty much."[3] She and Nan understood that boys would be boys. They once overturned Marion's boat in the water. She didn't like it, but she didn't refuse to let them use it afterward. Was Eleanor as lenient? Did Marion and Nan compete with her for the children's attention?

The 1920s was an extremely busy decade for the Roosevelts, and it is no wonder that the children felt neglected by their parents. Eleanor and Franklin were often out of town, and the children were left with Granny, which was a good thing for them because she was affectionate and constant, if overindulgent. Why a mother gets blamed for neglect and a father does not is a book unto itself. The boys became increasingly quarrelsome with one another, and Eleanor tried to stay out of the way. Franklin tolerated their dinner-table discussions with great jocularity. Eleanor must have left the table in anger and tears on more than one occasion. She wrote Marion and Nan that the boys made her feel stupid when she tried to discuss a subject they thought she knew nothing about. During a lunch with Rose Schneiderman and Maud Swartz at Campobello, Eleanor had spoken freely of her interest in trade unions. Later she wrote Marion and Nan, "I was left as I always am with the boys, feeling quite impotent to make a dent. . . . [They] regard me as a woman to be dutifully and affectionately thought of because I am their mother, but . . . I hold queer opinions [that] can't be considered seriously as against those of their usual male environment!" Rose later wrote in her autobiography that Eleanor was "a born trade unionist."[4] Marion and Nan were often at such family dinners and heard the discussions. If they defended Eleanor, neither Marion nor Eleanor ever said so.

On an evening at the dinner table at Springwood in 1929, as Marion described in her interview many years later, there was a disagreement with Mama because Eleanor announced her intention to take the younger boys and drive with Marion and Nan in their own car on a European tour. Sara thought that mode of travel was unacceptable for the governor's wife. When Brud said that if his mother drove she would probably land them in a ditch, Eleanor left the table in tears, and FDR sent the boy to apologize to his mother. Eleanor returned and then agreed that Nan and Marion would take their Buick and she would rent a car and driver, satisfying her mother-in-law and casting a shadow over the trip. Marion reported the disagreement in an interview, but she did not say that she followed Eleanor out of the room to wipe away Eleanor's tears. Instead, Marion said, "Brother paid very dearly for that remark. Eleanor could be very hard."[5] Marion and Nan were privy to the innermost workings of the Roosevelt family, which put them at both an advantage and a disadvantage. They had reason to feel like insiders; at the same time, they were wary of making someone angry and risking their favored places.

As far as we know from what Marion said, she generally did not take Eleanor's side in arguments. She was inclined, however, to defend Franklin and Granny. Indeed, Marion's remembrances are curiously lacking in sympathy for Eleanor. It is Franklin's good humor, courage, and broad-mindedness that Marion singled out for special commendation. (This attitude is frequently borne out in interviews with Marion cited in Kenneth Davis's *Invincible Summer*.) She applauded, for example, Franklin sending Brud to apologize to his mother for insulting her and telling him to bring her back to the table. Perhaps Marion and Nan knew to leave well enough alone. Or perhaps that night was one of the times when Eleanor went back to the cottage and spent the night talking with Marion and Nan, being consoled there.

Marion's relationship with the boys reached a turning point in the summer of 1929 on the trip to Europe. Brud was celebrating his fifteenth birthday, and John was thirteen. The women's ages did not much matter—the boys thought they were all the same: old (Marion was thirty-nine; Eleanor and Nan were forty-five). The problem was that the teenage boys had three "mothers" along—not exactly a formula for an easy family vacation.[6]

Eleanor angrily acceded to Granny's demands and rented (and paid for) a fine car and chauffeur to travel with Brud and John through Europe; Marion and Nan had their car shipped over to drive themselves. All travel with family is challenging, and Eleanor had already been unnerved by Mama's insistence that they travel first class as befitted the family of the governor of New York. The journey thus started out on a false note for Eleanor. (The first steps in a trip usually set the stage, don't they?) As the trip progressed, Marion played up to the boys, until finally Eleanor agreed to let Marion celebrate Brud's birthday (17 August) by having him drive alone with her in her car, with Eleanor, John, and Nan going in the other car.

Marion remembered the trip as adventurous. The boys themselves seem never to have spoken of traveling with Marion and Nan, although usually they were asked only about their parents. They argued and fought all along the way, which unsettled Eleanor. Marion simply remembered it as the normal behavior of active boys, and she never lost her love for young Franklin. She did arrange a magical evening in which she hired a boatman to take the group to Mont St. Michel as the tide came in. It was close to a religious experience for the three women. They remembered Eleanor having had read Henry Adams's *Mont St. Michel and Chartres* aloud to them at Campobello.

But such happy moments were few. When the summer ended and

the women and boys came home, Eleanor said she would never do it again; and indeed, it was the friends' last trip with the boys. The demands the trip placed on their friendship were heavy—three women not in complete agreement about how to handle teenage boys, and Marion eager to have her own special experience with Brud on his birthday. Eleanor was left feeling like a spoilsport, a role she sometimes assigned herself. Eleanor later took her grandchildren with her on various world trips, and they were enchanted. By then Eleanor was full of confidence as a famous traveler, and the children treasured the special time with their grandmother. So perhaps the journey in 1929 was not really wasted time—Eleanor's mistakes with her own children led her to play a more confident role with her grandchildren.

After Marion and Nan had moved to Connecticut, Eleanor's son John and his wife, Anne, and their children lived in the cottage. When their first two children, Nina and Haven, contracted polio (1952), they were moved next door to their grandmother's house, where she insisted that they be cared for by her doctor, David Gurewitsch. Nina became especially close to her grandmother and to Dr. Gurewitsch, who continued to treat her after they moved to New York City. She especially remembered summer visits to Val-Kill and the time her grandmother took her and numerous cousins for a picnic on the nearby estate of a Livingston relative (Eleanor was kin to the Livingstons on her mother's side of the family; one of the most famous was Robert Livingston, a member of a wealthy Hudson Valley family and a signer of the Declaration of Independence). When Eleanor knocked on the Livingstons' door, Mrs. Livingston shouted, "Go away, Eleanor!" "I so well remember the veiled surprise on my grandmother's face," Nina said, "but, never one to be daunted by small inconveniences; we were to have our lovely picnic regardless of Mrs. Livingston having forgotten that she had invited us in the first place."[7] They drove down a dirt road toward the river and found their own picnic spot. And thus a lesson about not being "daunted by small inconveniences" surfaced in memory more than a half-century later.

10

VAL-KILL INDUSTRIES

The cottage was not an end in itself. —Eleanor Roosevelt

Val-Kill was not just a weekend retreat. It was an accommodating community where women could meet and talk over a range of interests. The three friends worked together on a number of significant projects, and they started early. In 1925 Eleanor, Marion, and Nan, along with Elinor Morgenthau and Caroline O'Day, took over a mimeographed bulletin from the New York Democratic Women's Division with its office in New York City and turned it into a monthly magazine, the *Women's Democratic News*.[1] All the women at one time or another suggested topics, wrote articles, and served as editors. They soon encountered interference, especially from Louis Howe, who liked to run things for FDR's benefit, so they learned to do it all themselves—to make up a dummy, proofread, and take it to press. Eleanor proved to be a successful fund raiser, selling ads to support the publication. Each of the women wrote columns under her own byline, describing their various activities. The favorite feature was a regular article from one of the women called "Trooping for Democracy," which was about their travels to organize local Democratic chapters in the state.

In her November 1925 column Caroline O'Day wrote to readers, "When politics is through with us we are retiring to this charming retreat that is now rearing its stone walls against the beautiful cedars of a Dutchess County hillside. Here we mean to embark on an absolutely new enterprise."[2] This is a rather mysterious comment because there is no other evidence that Caroline ever intended to live at Val-Kill (her papers have never been archived). She was a delegate to Democratic Party national conventions and was active in many of the same women's organizations as Eleanor, Marion, and Nan. She shared Eleanor's peace sentiments and carried them further—she was an ardent pacifist. Her most ambitious undertaking still lay ahead in 1934, when she would be elected to Congress as an at-large New York representative. She would serve four terms. She and Marion, who looked somewhat alike with their long, serious faces and dark dresses, were close friends and often met for lunch when both were in the city.

Caroline must have been caught up in the free spirit of Val-Kill to make its existence so public. What holds our attention is the language itself: nowhere do we find Val-Kill more handsomely described. If we take her at her word, we must assume that she was thinking of it as a "retreat." We can only speculate that the four women were considering living together, and that in itself suggests that they were thinking of the cottage on the Val-Kill as a place for women to live communally. Although Caroline was to spend nights there, she never made it the home that Eleanor, Marion, and Nan did. But clearly she thought about it, which is sometimes the way of a woman's expansive and private dreams. Presumably, "the absolutely new enterprise" that she mentioned was Val-Kill Industries, the furniture factory that the women would build next door to the cottage. Caroline would go on to serve as a sort of "honorary" vice-president, contribute financially to the business, and write articles to publicize their efforts.

Val-Kill Industries was meant to address a growing problem. Although the Great Depression was still several years away, there was already a pressing need in Dutchess County and other rural districts to provide jobs for young men to keep them from leaving their family farms, an ideal that was never very successful. Nan thought that perhaps the men could be trained to make high-quality reproduction American furniture; in time, women would be employed in the weaving shop. The colonial revival and arts and crafts movements had demonstrated a national interest in finely crafted furniture, and the three women saw an opportunity to exploit that interest, to create local jobs, and to help keep rural America intact. Val-Kill Industries would produce a decade of crafts that remain American collectibles.

The shop at Val-Kill was a bold enterprise, with Nan as the "driving spirit" behind it.[3] She had woodworking skills and loved to make things (Eleanor said, in a statement that is often quoted, that Nan could do "anything with her hands"), and Eleanor had the necessary contacts and was excellent at promoting others (an early brochure described the enterprise as "Val-Kill Shop, Roosevelt Industries, Hyde Park, New York"). The first sign of what Nan intended appears on early blueprints as a small workshop inside the cottage itself, but that limited idea was abandoned as Nan's ambitions developed. Instead, the women built a separate two-story cinder-block building about two hundred feet from the cottage that would be expanded as the business grew. Although the women had shared equally in the costs of the cottage, Eleanor assumed the major costs of constructing the shop building, and Nan selected the equipment from New York suppliers. In search of furniture designs, Nan, Eleanor, and Marion went to the Metropolitan Museum of Art to learn from the master curators of American design. Morris Schwartz, an authority on restoring early American furniture, took a personal interest in the women's plans and visited the shop several times to encourage Nan and her staff.

Nan developed recipes for stains and an elaborate finishing process to give furniture a special sheen, and she sketched drafts for individual pieces that a part-time draftsman converted into blueprints and templates. She set out to hire the best wood craftsmen she could find, and her first three hires were exceptional. On Christmas Day 1926 she was able to persuade Frank Salvatore Landolfa to move from New York City and join the Val-Kill shop. He was an Italian immigrant from a family of cabinetmakers and woodworkers who had met Eleanor Roosevelt when he was a teacher in a vocational program in New York. He and Nan bought machinery and workbenches and set up the shop in early 1927. His first job was to make furniture for the cottage. To alleviate his misgivings about leaving behind his life in the city, Eleanor arranged for him to take a night class to learn to speak better English and provided him with room and board and driving lessons for a car she helped him purchase.

The second skilled woodworker Nan hired was Otto Berge, a self-taught cabinetmaker who had come to Long Island from Norway in 1913. Nan interviewed him in New York City and hired him, and he came to work at the shop in the summer of 1927. He was especially proud of the chest-on-chest he made for the White House during the first year of FDR's presidency. He regarded himself, not Nan, as the master craftsman and took great pride in quality craftsmanship. He did not think Nan was a skilled craftsman or even ran a good shop, but he did not complain to Mrs. Roosevelt, knowing that she would never think anything wrong about a friend. However, he was thrust into the middle of a conflict between Mrs. Roosevelt and Nan when Eleanor rejected frames that she had ordered as gifts because they were not made out of old wood from the White House, as she had requested. It was the occasion for a quarrelsome exchange of letters between Eleanor and Nan, who insisted that Berge had used old wood. When Mrs. Roosevelt returned to Val-Kill and discussed things with Berge, he told her that Nan had always known that the wood was new and that she had required him to make the frames anyway. In an interview years later, Berge described his dislike of Nan and his belief that he had opened Eleanor's eyes to Nan's failures. Whether or not Berge's complaints, as documented in the interview, influenced Eleanor's later decision to close the shop cannot be documented.

Eleanor was a great favorite with Berge. He liked for her to wander down from the cottage to watch him work in the shop, which Marion described as "light and airy and filled with the pungent odor of wood." Berge admired Mrs. Roosevelt, "so broad minded and so fair and square, an extremely intelligent personality." He was especially impressed that she didn't mind that he was a Republican.[4]

To this team Nan added Matthew Famiglietti, a friend of Landolfa's from the vocational school, to manage the finishing room. Although the shop did hire local boys from time to time, the industry never was able to attract enough of them to fulfill the women's hopes of keeping young men employed in the country. Although records are incomplete, at its highest level Val-Kill hired some eighteen employees.

In 1934, when the women decided to add weaving to their enterprise, they went to Asheville, North Carolina, to study the Biltmore weaving shop operated by Fred Seeley, who had taken it over when Mrs. Vanderbilt had given up her projects at Biltmore. Seeley had some twenty weavers who wove homespun, which they dyed with special natural dyes. Seeley gave the women a loom and also offered to provide instruction for anyone they wanted to send to learn as his guest. When they returned to Val-Kill, they discovered that Nelly Johannesen, a Swedish woman familiar with handicrafts who had opened a tearoom at the entrance to Val-Kill the previous year, was eager to learn to weave. When Eleanor told her about the opportunity to travel to Asheville, she wanted to go. It was a turning point in Nelly's life. She learned to make cloth, including some used in making suits for the president. Her weaving enterprise was mostly independent of the furniture shop, but it gave an added attraction to Val-Kill.

Next, Val-Kill workers started a forge run by Otto Berge's brother, Arnold. He and his two assistants turned out more than fifty items, mostly pewter—porringers, matchbox covers, plates, cups, cheese slicers, lamps, cups, inkwells, vases—everything stamped with the Val-Kill name. In all these ways—training craftsmen, producing quality products, and developing a center of activities in a rural part of the state—Val-Kill was an amazing success for much of a decade, during the most challenging economic times in American history. That four women without much business experience defied the odds against them is in itself a feminist story.

•

Val-Kill Industries started off going full steam. In addition to making the furniture for Stone Cottage, it was time to make furniture for Franklin's new cottage in Warm Springs. Nan went to Georgia to consult with Franklin about what he would need and returned with plans to build Val-Kill pieces for him. Knowing FDR's admiration for Thomas Jefferson, Eleanor, Marion, and Nan went to Jefferson's home in Monticello and were impressed by a special chair and table Jefferson used when making his drawings. The table had a second top that could be turned so that Jefferson did not have to stand to see his plans from the opposite side. Nan realized that such a table and chair would enable Franklin to work in a similar manner, and she received permission to make special drawings so that she could reproduce both the table and the chair, which are now in the Little White House at Warm Springs. They also were allowed to borrow Jefferson's music rack, which Nan used to design several reproductions to be used as magazine racks. In a visit to Campobello in the summer of 1936 Eleanor wrote in her 24 July "My Day" column about the pleasure of watching Miss Cook and Miss Dickerman rearranging what Eleanor called the children's "old school room" with Val-Kill furniture.

Nan sometimes invited prospective Val-Kill furniture buyers to Stone Cottage to see Val-Kill furniture in an ideal setting that encouraged individuality. The women were willing to sacrifice some privacy in order to show off the furniture, and as a bonus buyers got to see the way the three friends lived. Visitors looking at the 1933 photograph of the living room at the stone house would probably have agreed that it was a room they would like to have in their own houses.

Elinor and Henry Morgenthau sent in a big order for furniture, as did Caroline O'Day; Sara Delano Roosevelt ordered tables for the James Roosevelt Memorial Library in Hyde Park. The shop also made furniture for the children's room in the National History Museum in Buffalo. Throughout the 1930s, Eleanor, writing on White House stationery, ordered furniture, pewter, and small wooden pieces that bore the president's seal, instructing Nan to send them as gifts to various family members and friends. There wasn't a business like it in America; almost overnight the shop's products, sponsored by the First Lady in the White House, were in the public eye.

It was a heady time. Newspaper and magazine reporters enjoyed featuring articles about Val-Kill, highlighting the fact that it was a business owned by Mrs. Franklin D. Roosevelt and making small mention of the other partners. Eleanor often opened her house on East 65th Street in New York City to exhibit the furniture. There was a display store at 331 Madison Avenue (not coincidentally, the office of the Women's Division of the New York State Democratic Committee), and furniture was exhibited at the Bush Terminal Sales Building, the Macbeth Gallery, and the Elsie de Wolf shop. The fact that Val-Kill furniture was modeled on pieces from the collection of the Metropolitan Museum and exhibited in art galleries reinforced its aesthetic importance. For nine years, from 1927 through 1936, Val-Kill sold to department stores, direct from the factory, through catalog sales, and at the annual New York City sale.

Although the American arts and crafts movement was in decline by the 1930s, there were still currents of interest, and Nan's shop put Val-Kill on the map for its reproductions of early American furniture. Today Val-Kill furniture is as scarce as hen's teeth, and collectors scour the Internet looking for butterfly drop-leaf tables, walnut gate-leg tables, a desk-on-frame, leather-upholstered Cromwell chairs, trestle tables, desks, chests, mirrors, dressing tables, and pewter. Some pieces are on public display today in Stone Cottage and at the Franklin D. Roosevelt Presidential Library and Museum in Hyde Park, and the principal collector, Richard Cain, maintains an active website. At Val-Kill, Eleanor and Nan had become businesswomen with practical experience, although Nan's focus was on the furniture itself. Any profits they made, and these were small, were returned to the business. Eleanor was not out to make money, but she liked what she could do with it. In her autobiography she explained that the money she earned writing and in radio work enabled her to do many things on her own. She used most of the money she earned to fund her favorite projects. When she began seeing what her money could do, the struggle to keep Val-Kill Industries going at anything like full capacity began to weigh on her.

Historians of the New Deal also point out that Eleanor Roosevelt's experiences at Val-Kill led to her advocacy for national programs in arts and crafts that became part of the New Deal's cultural outreach. She took Nan many times to the New Deal community in Arthurdale, West Virginia, the federal resettlement project that has been called "Eleanor's Little Village," where Nan gave instructions on starting a craft shop.[5] Isabella Greenway, in the same year that Eleanor, Marion, and Nan founded Val-Kill Industries, founded Arizona Hut, where World War I veterans made furniture and their wives made needle-point products to supplement their pensions. Isabella, like Eleanor, purchased herself most of the furniture made in her shop, and in 1930 she used much of it to open her new enterprise, the Arizona Inn in Tucson, which is family-operated today.

Although FDR is credited with having encouraged his "gang" to start a furniture factory to give employment to local boys and men to supplement their farm income and keep them from leaving for jobs elsewhere, those who worked at Val-Kill Industries did not think he ever took much of an interest in what they were doing. The idea, however, was consistent with FDR's experiments to give employment to local workers. In this way Val-Kill Industries was a precursor to other New Deal projects. Although it closed after almost a decade, it deserves a place in women's history at a time when few women had opportunities to become entrepreneurs.

11

THE TODHUNTER SCHOOL

Even in those days, you knew [Eleanor Roosevelt] was a great woman.
— Anne Ward Gilbert

In 1927, five years after Marion had begun teaching English at the Todhunter School on New York's East Side, she approached Eleanor with an idea that they go into partnership together and buy the school. The director at the time, Winifred Todhunter, had purchased the private school for girls in 1921 and renamed it; now she was ready to retire and return to her native England. She asked Marion, her vice principal, if she wanted to acquire the school, and Marion, who knew how important Allenswood had been to Eleanor when she was young, rushed to sound her out on that possibility. As an experienced administrator Marion knew a good teacher when she saw one, and she believed that Eleanor Roosevelt was a "natural." Later in her White House press conferences for women, reporters admired the way in which Eleanor Roosevelt opened up the conferences for questions and answers, like a classroom.

Miss Todhunter, an Oxford University graduate, had given the Todhunter School a reputation for progressive teaching that emphasized a college preparatory program as well as courses in the arts. Students, daughters of privilege, mostly from neighborhoods bordered by Park Avenue and Central Park, were enrolled from primary grades through high school. Although most of the other elite schools did not admit Jewish girls, Todhunter had a small number, including two who were elected by their classmates to head the upper and lower schools.[1] The faculty were women with career ambitions, some of them graduates of the best colleges. One was Margaret Clapp, whom Marion urged to continue her graduate education. Clapp taught English literature at the Todhunter School for twelve years while working on her master's degree, which she obtained from Columbia University in 1937. She went on to teach at City College of New York, Douglass College, Columbia University, and Brooklyn College. In 1949 she became president of Wellesley College, her alma mater. Marion was sometimes overlooked as sitting quietly in the corner (Frances Perkins said so), but she had a good eye for picking leaders.

Eleanor was thrilled to hear Marion's proposal. She agreed immediately to form a partnership with Marion and Nan as the owners of Todhunter. (Nan's partnership was in name only; her job was at the New York Democratic Women's office and at the Val-Kill furniture factory.) The stationery was imprinted with the school's new leadership:

The Todhunter School
66 East 80th Street, New York City,
Telephone: Rhinelander 6478
Honorary Principal, Miss W. A. Todhunter;
Principal, Miss Marion Dickerman;
Associate Principal, Mrs. Franklin D. Roosevelt

There was no mistaking that last name. But if having Eleanor join the school meant a good deal to Marion, it also engendered some controversy because most of the girls' families were Republicans, some with outright disdain for FDR's politics. On balance, however, the Roosevelt name would give immediate distinction to Todhunter, and Marion was eager to make it happen.

Eleanor's letter in response to Marion's proposal about the school, written while she was with Franklin and his friends (unhappily) on the *Larooco* houseboat in Florida, revealed a good deal about Eleanor's growing ambitions for what she might learn to do. She immediately addressed her concerns:

> I think you ought to take the 1st place for the first year with the understanding that you have no financial responsibility. It will be easier for you to settle in that way & when Miss Todhunter and Miss Burrell [presumably Todhunter's colleague] depart, then

I'll slip in & do all I can for you but I feel strongly that you have to find out gradually what I can do. The one or two afternoons a week sound easy & I'll talk over the course with you but associate principals for the good of the school should have college degrees & I think I'd better be something less high sounding! I'd rather not have any financial consideration enter into the first year as I would consider that I was being paid in experience and the next year if we assumed joint financial responsibility then we could arrange some percent of profit after your salary & all expenses were paid. I think it will be quite thrilling for it is your gift & it would be a crime for you not to use it & I know you can make a great success. It is going to be such fun to work with you & Nan & you are dears to let me join in it all for I'd never have had the initiative or the ability in any one line to have done anything interesting alone![2]

Eleanor taught the older girls, believing it was harder to teach young children, and she gave courses in American history, English and American literature, and current events. Her six years at Todhunter were some of the happiest of her life. "I like it better than anything else I do," she told a reporter, this despite that after Franklin was elected governor in 1928 and again in 1930 she had to commute from Albany to the city two and a half days a week, which even she admitted was strenuous. When the legislature was not in session, she commuted from Hyde Park. She left by train Sunday night, went to Todhunter Monday, Tuesday, and a half-day on Wednesday, returned to the house on East 65th Street to catch up on other work, and took a train back to Albany in time to host an afternoon open house at the governor's mansion. In her absence Missy LeHand, FDR's secretary, was hostess at Albany and had everything ready for Eleanor to step in and serve as the governor's First Lady. Often Eleanor and Marion made the trip together, catching up on school news. Although Eleanor had learned to drop off quickly for short naps when she was traveling, she frequently had to grade batches of papers.

One of the happiest days of Eleanor's Todhunter life was in the fall of 1932 when she took her first grandchild, Anna's daughter, Ellie, to enroll in the first grade. Eleanor's students were always on her mind—in letters to Franklin she complained when they weren't doing well and wondered how as their teacher she could do better. Among the most distinctive aspects of her classes, for those whose parents allowed it, were visits to city courts and tenement districts, where the students spent hours listening and learning. She wanted to expose them to lives unlike their own and to make the government "real and alive" for them. Like Mlle. Souvestre of Allenswood in England, she demanded that her students think for themselves and not simply give back what they heard her say or what they had read in their textbooks. These field trips became the most memorable aspects of the students' years at Todhunter. In addition to teaching, Eleanor met with students and parents and hosted lunches for school anniversaries. After FDR was elected president, she withdrew from the faculty, but she sometimes offered a class for graduates and their friends. As regularly as clockwork she arranged trips for Todhunter faculty and students to come to the White House and tour the Capitol.

Eleanor loved teaching, and she was very good at it. She taught small classes and gave the students a lot of personal attention, and they loved her. In the mornings Mrs. Roosevelt and Miss Dickerman, robed in academic gowns, greeted the girls as they entered the building. Eleanor was both intellectually and emotionally engaged with the students, as dominant a figure as Mlle. Souvestre had been at Allenswood. She wanted to pass along the legacy of her great teacher, and she did. She had rigorous standards and was a tough grader. She challenged her students' assumptions and prejudices, telling them, "Learn new things and see new things with your own eyes." Her teaching had tapped into one of the "real springs of life."[3]

Anne Ward (Gilbert) lived right across the street from the Roosevelts on East 65th, and she and her family were often asked over to dinner. When Anne enrolled at Todhunter School she studied history and drama with Mrs. Roosevelt. "She was absolutely fantastic—the way to learn, and the willingness to learn, and everything. And she was so vivacious. . . . I think anybody who had her as a teacher or as a friend learned so much and received so much from her. . . . She was always nervous, always shy, even when she was teaching. You could tell. She was very humble. . . . Even in those days you knew she was a great woman."[4] Anne also admired Marion Dickerman and insisted that she never saw any "hard feelings" between Mrs. Roosevelt and Miss Dickerman. After graduating in 1928 from Todhunter, Anne continued to stay in touch with both women. After Mrs. Roosevelt's death and the children's sale of the Roosevelt property, Anne's family auction business in Garrison, New York, handled an estate sale.

12

THE WHITE HOUSE

The more you live in a "gold-fish bowl," the less people really know about you!
—Eleanor Roosevelt

After FDR's election as president, Eleanor had decidedly mixed feelings. Glad for him that he had fulfilled his ambition, she nevertheless feared that moving to the White House meant giving up her own freedom. As she spent more of her time away from Val-Kill, Marion and Nan could not help her as often, and they were to feel the loss more deeply than Eleanor, who, after all, had much to attend to. She had become adept at managing a schedule that defies easy understanding even today.[1] She found help in confronting her fears by stepping out on her own. She did this most effectively in the way she had learned to do, by quickly making a new friend—Lorena Hickok, called "Hick," an Associated Press reporter assigned her during the last month of FDR's presidential campaign. They were very different in background. Hick's was working class, and she was a seasoned professional journalist. She knew the ways of newspaper people, and she could help Mrs. Roosevelt negotiate the terrain. Then, as they spent time together on the campaign trail, they began to share stories of their unhappy childhoods. Very quickly they recognized in each other the need for friendship. Perhaps the most astute "reading" of Eleanor Roosevelt at the time of FDR's first term was Hickok's immediate recognition (watching her expressions in public) that Mrs. Roosevelt was a "reluctant First Lady." Sensing Eleanor's vulnerability made it easy for Hick to know her needs. "Mrs. R.," as Hick often called her, was open and generous. An intimate relationship began that was to change over time, but their loyalty to one another never wavered.[2]

Those who remembered Eleanor's debut as a speaker at Nan's 1922 fund-raiser found the difference in her self-confidence remarkable.

By the end of FDR's four years as governor she had earned a life—teaching, meeting, writing, and speaking. Even before she realized it herself, her friends had begun to note changes in her—she was less available. As FDR's presidential campaign began to heat up, Eleanor realized that her life was going to change in ways she did not want. By the time Louis Howe and FDR had put together FDR's first run for the presidency in 1932, however—a story that others have told many times in many places—Eleanor was a central player in a game she had mastered, making political connections for FDR wherever she went. She insisted that she was doing it only for FDR, but she loved the opportunities it gave her to do the things she wanted to do. Nevertheless, when she actually faced being First Lady, she certainly had qualms about living under the relentless scrutiny of the public. She would compensate for what she viewed as her confinement by having frequent overnight guests to the White House and by traveling a great deal in behalf of causes to make better the lives of the least, and by not paying much attention to her critics. There was never a First Lady with the energy, courage, and determination of Eleanor Roosevelt, and perhaps there never will be. She was not captive to the title, and her own personal suffering made her more sensitive to the lives of others she hoped to represent.

Marion and Nan may have believed that the transition into public life was going to be seamless for them and that the friendship would remain unchanged. They loved being part of FDR's inner circle. When FDR and Howe made them members of the select Cuff Links gang (each initiate received a pair of gold cufflinks for having worked in FDR's 1920 vice-presidential campaign), they knew they were consummate insiders. They hosted annual anniversary dinners for the group and celebrated FDR's fifty-first birthday in January 1933, before his first presidential inauguration. The birthday party was held in the big room at the cottage in an extravagant affair planned by Howe with cocktail "glasses, glasses, glasses," Marion remembered.[3]

During the week leading up to the 1932 Democratic Convention in Chicago, as FDR was preparing to win the nomination, Marion and

Nan had been party to one of the best-kept secrets in Eleanor's history—one Marion revealed many years after Eleanor's death.[4] Eleanor wrote a letter to Nan saying that she would not give up her personal life so that FDR could be president. Nan was to give the letter to Howe when she saw him before the convention. When Howe read the letter, he was dumbfounded. He tore it in shreds and told Nan that she was never to speak of the contents. In telling Kenneth Davis about the incident many years later, Marion reported that Eleanor had said she would marry Earl Miller, but Marion asked Davis not to use his name. He did not mention Miller when relating the incident in *Invincible Summer*, but he did name him in *FDR: The New York Years*, which was published after Marion had died. Whatever the truth of that threat, Eleanor had made clear to Marion and Nan that she was frightened at the prospect of being First Lady. They, on the other hand, gloried in the triumph of the long campaign to make FDR president. Perhaps they had not anticipated that as Eleanor changed the environment that she found inhospitable and put her own stamp on the White House, she would also change her inner circle. Perhaps Marion and Nan were willing to give up the quiet evenings by the fire at Val-Kill in exchange for evenings at the White House, near the center of political power. However, as the intimate circle of Eleanor, Marion, Nan, and Franklin changed and many other friends and associates became constant visitors, more and more Marion and Nan were on the fringes.

The differences among Eleanor and Marion and Nan widened after the Roosevelts moved to Washington, and Eleanor was swept along by her own advice to her students to learn new things and see with new eyes. The Roosevelt White House was a welcoming place to family, friends, and visitors of every kind, and when Eleanor invited them, they showed up—even strangers she had met on the street. It was just as FDR and Eleanor wanted it, like the fun-filled, family-filled White House during the Theodore Roosevelt years. Although FDR would often yearn to go home to the Hudson Valley, he also had advantages in the White House: a large staff to wait on him, a new regulation swimming pool in the basement, an operated elevator, large living quarters with a private office upstairs, and Missy LeHand, called the "gatekeeper" for controlling access to FDR, available always when he needed her. There were guest rooms for friends, some of them permanent guests (Louis Howe; Harry Hopkins, FDR's director of New Deal relief programs and a security adviser during World War II; and Lorena Hickok); a place to watch movies and be entertained at home by invited artists (Lily Pons gave the first concert; Cornelia Otis Skinner performed a monologue); and when his friends sent him gifts of foods he loved (wild game especially), he could avoid the bland fare of Henrietta Nesbitt's kitchen. FDR's second-floor office with its cluttered desk was a comfortable place where Missy invited guests to sit on sofas and chairs while FDR filled their drink orders and leaned back and talked and laughed. Eleanor was sometimes included, sometimes not, and often she was out with her own friends. Or Missy could have supper brought in for her and "Eff Dee," as she called FDR, or for a small group of close friends.[5] In good weather lunch was served downstairs on the south porch for Franklin and Eleanor and guests, and picnics were held on the lawn, when the U.S. Marine Band played on special occasions.

The Roosevelt children took advantage of everything (including their parents)—and if they bridled when asked for identification when they first came to the White House, it wasn't long before the staff recognized them, their husbands and girl friends and wives, their children, and their friends. They received favored treatment and were indulged. On New Year's Day 1936, two of FDR's sons studying at Harvard invited two of their professors to discuss politics and spend the night in the White House, and Eleanor reported on it in a "My Day" column. For her part, Eleanor showed her boys how to raid the icebox (and also showed Amelia Earhart, who was embarrassed to have been quoted as saying she had gone hungry staying overnight at the White House).

For the rest of their lives some of the Roosevelt grandchildren would remember inaugurations, birthdays, Christmases, and long stays of every kind in the White House. Their grandfather was president of the United States, but he still read aloud to them from Dickens's *A Christmas Carol* and handed out their Christmas presents. And they could look enviously at all the things he kept on his desk—a clutter of the useful (pens, clocks) and the useless (Democratic donkey and Republican elephant figures)—but they were Papa's toys, an intriguing notion to a young child.

However, the White House cramped the style of Eleanor Roosevelt, who called it a "museum." She had been developing toward the moment when she could exert her independence, and now it seemed about to be taken away from her. She didn't want to be shadowed by the Secret Service, and she wanted to drive her own car, take herself up and down on the elevator, rearrange her own furniture, and come and go as she pleased without being checked in and checked out, her whereabouts recorded in a daily log. She also liked to carry her own bag and to travel anonymously. She was interested in everything, she wanted to represent those who had no representation, and she wanted to be free. Being FDR's "eyes and ears"—as was often said about her usefulness for a man confined to a wheelchair—to get out and see how Americans were faring during the Great Depression was a built-in reason to do all those things. And those reports from his "Missus" gave FDR a way of keeping up with people and places in America and with Eleanor, and he didn't seem to mind that she set her own schedule. In fact, he welcomed not having her always insisting upon her causes. After 1935, friends who saw her less could read in her "My Day" column what she was up to. She invited guests to the White House to be taken care of by the staff whether she was in residence or not. In the White House or on the road, she often had Hick as her closest companion. Unlike Marion and Nan, Hick did not court favor with the president, which was perhaps one of her attractions for Eleanor.

•

Mrs. Roosevelt told her followers what she thought of living in the White House. For readers of her 7 January 1936 "My Day" column, she explained,

There is, however, one consolation to any one who lives in the public eye, namely, that while it may be most difficult to keep the world from knowing where you dine and what you eat and what you wear, so much interest is focused on these somewhat unimportant things, that you are really left completely free to live your own inner life as you wish. And, thank God, few people are so poor that they do not have an inner life which feeds the real springs of thought and action. So if I may offer a thought in consolation to others who for a time have to live in a "gold-fish bowl," it is: "Don't worry because people know all that you do, for the really important things about anyone is what they are and what they think and feel and the more you live in a 'gold-fish bowl,' the less people really know about you!"

Not everything had changed, however, for Eleanor, moving into the White House had been akin in one way to moving into the New York governor's mansion: Marion and Nan showed up to help settle her in. After the 1933 presidential inauguration, Marion returned to Todhunter and Nan stayed another week. A story in the Washington newspaper reported that Mrs. Roosevelt had been seen wandering through the inaugural grandstand (it had rained) looking for Miss Dickerman and Miss Cook to make sure they had good seats. Although Eleanor had many guests to look after that day, she had invited all the faculty and students from Todhunter as well, even though she was not still their teacher.

Nan helped Eleanor dismantle the Hoover White House and decided what had to go and what Eleanor needed: a long bed for FDR, which she would design and have made in the Val-Kill shop, as well as a bed for Eleanor and other pieces of Val-Kill furniture. She helped to hang some of the hundreds of framed photographs that Eleanor had in her bedroom and sitting room, to position her desk and table where Eleanor and Tommy could work, and to make a comfortable place before the fire to read or listen to the radio (there were seven fireplaces in the White House). And she left an uncluttered view out the window to the Washington Monument, where a blinking red light at night was a beacon of comfort for Eleanor. Marion's and Nan's names regularly turn up in official White House records as overnight houseguests, as do many others. They did not all know or like one another, but they didn't have to. Eleanor was an impresario when it came to managing her guests.

The White House, in fact, became the Roosevelts' grand hotel, with every bed filled, visitors standing in line for receptions, FDR's children and grandchildren vying for his attention, and the White House staff trying to adjust to the changes. Eleanor met with them all— the reception crowds and the intimate dinners. As her interests and responsibilities changed, she saw less and less of Marion and Nan. She attended many public occasions, and Hick was consuming most of her private time. Over the next year they even talked of sharing a house, perhaps a reflection of Eleanor having learned how to live at Stone Cottage with Marion and Nan. And not long after the Roosevelts moved into the White House Hick gave up her journalism career to be close to Eleanor when she realized that she had lost her objectivity in reporting on the First Lady. On Eleanor's recommendation, she was given a federal job traveling across the country to report to Harry Hopkins on conditions during the Great Depression.

Although Eleanor invited Hick to Val-Kill, she seldom went and then only when Marion and Nan were not there. Hick was very possessive, and so were Marion and Nan. They vied for Eleanor's time and attention, and Hick was winning. Hick is missing in most photographs, one indication that at least some family members, perhaps, did not want her in the picture. Her friendship with Eleanor is not mentioned in any of Marion's and Nan's letters during the period. The written evidence that Eleanor continued her separate friendships with the three women, especially during FDR's first term, however, is in the official White House record, which shows how closely their visits overlapped.

When Eleanor reached the White House, Hick advised her about meeting the media and the public: she proposed that the First Lady host her own ladies-only press conferences, and Eleanor's letters to her about her activities became the basis for her "My Day" columns. The column became enormously popular and, not insignificantly, earned Eleanor some money. Eleanor rapidly developed political allies—and critics—among FDR's associates, and she spent so many nights away from the White House that it became a joke with reporters. She and Tommy, who had worked with her since 1922, traveled together an estimated 40,000 miles annually during FDR's first two terms. On the rare times when Eleanor traveled without Tommy, she often wrote. After years of building trust, Eleanor once advised Tommy, "Remember also that if you think anyone should be hired or fired you have my entire confidence, and I want you to act as you think wise." [6] Tommy was indispensable to Eleanor: "The person who makes life possible for me." [7] Together they answered the letters that poured in daily when Mrs. Roosevelt invited Americans to "write to me." She carried her letter bags everywhere, dictating on trains and planes, still at work at her desk until the early hours of the morning. In addition to her official correspondence—and she wanted every letter answered, if not by her then by someone to whom she forwarded it—she kept up a huge correspondence with her family and friends. Her letters to Marion and Nan became hastily dictated business notes, such as those that arranged for Marion to bring Todhunter students and faculty to the White House or ordered Val-Kill items to be made and sent as wedding gifts. Tommy knew that Esther and Elizabeth, Tommy's favorites, made no demands and offered their estate at Salt Meadow in Westport, Connecticut, as a sanctuary; Marion and Nan wanted Eleanor to themselves.

Stone Cottage changed in accord with Eleanor's new life. Marion and Nan had to adapt to remain part of FDR's inner circle in Washington politics. Eleanor saw how useful Nan could be in planning picnics at Val-Kill for FDR's political cronies. And Nan, for her part, found hosting picnics for the president and his friends heady, but exhausting. Now, when FDR and Eleanor came to Hyde Park from Washington, they brought crowds of visitors, many of them important presidential allies. Nan and Marion took care of many of the arrangements. Nan made a small portable grill to put by Franklin's chair so that he could cook meats the way he liked them (rare). She also became expert at preparing meals for large crowds. They counted on "Roosevelt weather"—the sunshine that often accompanied the president's visits and enabled them to have picnics. Nan planned the menus, ordered the food, and cooked. Eleanor admired the way Nan was able to do it all on a small budget.

Nan deserves special recognition for the role she played in organizing presidential picnics at Val-Kill for FDR and his friends, and Eleanor depended upon her to do it. When reporters wanted to know about the president's parties, they interviewed Nan, who relished the attention. She enjoyed describing the favorite dishes: pitchers of iced tea served with lemon and fresh mint, and fresh tomato juice; hot dogs (boiled or steamed the day before so they were ready to be broiled), hamburgers (mixed with a little salt pork), and steaks cooked on an outdoor grill; baked beans (soaked overnight); and, in early spring and fall, fish chowder. Her desserts included summer watermelon, ice cream, and Nelly Johannesen's cake with strawberries or chocolate sauce. "Miss Cook's cottage kitchen is her special pride," a local reporter noted, making no mention of either Marion or Eleanor, which must have been bracing to Nan.[8] Marion was also a well-prepared hostess—when Winston Churchill asked for whiskey, she was able to produce a bottle.

While Marion and Nan were proud to host such important occasions, they also became weary from Eleanor taking for granted that she could invite as many others as she chose. There was a price to be paid for being close to Eleanor and FDR: Marion and Nan increasingly were marginalized by very large, noisy, often jealous crowds of those with real power to influence the president and those who were just angling for it, often through Eleanor. Some of Eleanor's friends thought she was very discerning about people; others thought she could never spot a phony. Increasingly, Tommy ran interference for Mrs. R, whom she regarded as "just about the biggest person in the world. Anything I can do to help her—no matter what—justifies my existence."[9] At first Tommy liked Marion and Nan well enough, until they began to treat her as an obstacle to getting to Eleanor. Jealousies exploded. The dynamics of the friendship were changing. The friendship's base on the Val-Kill was wobbling, and harsh words lay in store for the "Three Graces."

•

FDR's election as president of the United States changed the private lives of everyone around him. Some were able to make the personal sacrifices that friendship with the Roosevelts required; some were not. Until his death in 1936 Louis Howe sacrificed his own personal life for theirs, able to befriend both FDR and Eleanor. With his death, each lost a wise adviser and a personal link that had brought them together. Missy's health suffered under the constancy of her long days and nights with FDR, and in 1941 she had a series of strokes that left her unable to work and deeply depressed. She died in July 1944—it was Eleanor, not Franklin, who visited her during her last terrible months; FDR apparently could not face it. Tommy Thompson gave up any personal life she may have wanted in order to serve Eleanor: her marriage to Frank Scheider ended in divorce in 1938 on grounds of voluntary separation (she was rarely home), and she never married her friend Henry Osthagen, though he was a frequent visitor at Val-Kill. Marion and Nan, on the other hand, were not prepared to sacrifice their own happiness.

One of Eleanor's closest friendships in the White House was with the young journalist and political activist Joseph Lash, her bridge to young voters, and the woman he married, Trude Pratt. When she first met Joe in 1939, when he and his compatriots were called before the House Committee on Un-American Activities, Eleanor was fifty-five years old and in her second term as First Lady. She understood that Joe and his friends were naïve and harbored leftist sentiments, but she did not run away from them or mind being branded a communist herself, as many liberals were. Joe was thirty and newly a partisan of FDR as director of the Youth Division of the National Democratic Committee—though FDR himself was angered by Joe's rude questions when Eleanor invited them to the White House. Eleanor loved Joe's youthful idealism, and he became a very close friend of hers, later in a position to become a leading Roosevelt scholar. Joe's (and his wife Trude's) close contacts in New York and Val-Kill put him in a position to know and see Eleanor's life in ways no others had been privileged. His interviews with some of her contemporaries are also invaluable historic documentation. Eleanor trusted him to tell the story as he knew it. His access to her history thus made him one of the most important Roosevelt scholars in a relationship that began with a unique friendship. Joe certainly took advantage of his opportunities, and it might be said that Eleanor took advantage of him. He benefited from knowing the president's family, and she benefited from the devotion of a young friend, more admiring of her than her own sons.

13

ARTHURDALE

Nothing we ever learn in this world is ever wasted and I have come to the conclusion that practically nothing we do ever stands by itself. — Eleanor Roosevelt

In the first one hundred days of the Roosevelt administration, excitement was in the air. Change was promised, and those who had suffered the most were encouraged to believe that the government would provide them with a better life. No one took more seriously the needs of the most desperate Americans than Eleanor Roosevelt. Hick kept Eleanor up-to-date on conditions with her nightly letters during her travels. She was especially horrified by the filth and squalor of the mining village at Scott's Run in West Virginia. She asked that Eleanor go see for herself. Immediately, Eleanor was at the wheel of her roadster and on the way to bring help.[1]

Eleanor kept readers of her "My Day" columns informed about her trips, alone or with friends, to see the first New Deal resettlement housing project near Morgantown, West Virginia. The trips required her to leave Washington on a night train, to fly on small planes in all kinds of weather (which never bothered her), and sometimes to drive alone along the narrow winding mountain roads, arriving in the dark to rush to a meeting waiting for her in the community center. She sometimes took meals in the homes of some of the residents. She came to know them by name and to care about their households. She cared more about the community that grew up, called Arthurdale for the family that sold the farm to the federal government, than any other single government program, reflecting as it did her concerns that something be done to provide housing, education, and jobs for the poorest Americans, already suffering from the squalid conditions of mining villages.

Hick, no stranger to childhood poverty, had been disturbed by the way families were living no better than animals in Scott's Run, named for the sewage stream (the only source of water) flowing through the center of the community of shacks. Eleanor had seen bad conditions in the New York City settlement houses where she volunteered after returning from school in London, and once during their courtship she had taken Franklin to see for himself. He was shocked, he said, never having known people lived that way, an impression that began to change the way the young man, considered to be something of a lightweight, looked at the world. FDR had already known that helping the neediest was going to be the focus of his first government programs, and at the top of the list was housing. As soon as Eleanor had seen Scott's Run she came home to tell FDR, and at the end of every trip to West Virginia and other federal housing projects she reported to the president on any progress being made. From the beginning many businessmen objected to federal appropriations for what they saw as the responsibility of the private sector, and if the mines failed and the miners lived in poverty, they expected the situation to be corrected by business interests — though starting factories in West Virginia mining towns was unlikely. Their ideas sounded good to some listeners, but Eleanor Roosevelt never kowtowed to the wealthy, and she seized the day. It wasn't going to be easy — there was a high incidence of illiteracy, the geography of the region was rough, and farming was unsuccessful in many of the rock-bound areas. And Eleanor's efforts to integrate blacks and Jews into the community of West Virginians met with stout opposition from some of the locals.

Eleanor always wanted to go into the homes of families she knew in Arthurdale to check on a sick child or to sit in the kitchen while a mother knitted and talked about the family. She insisted that the homes have indoor plumbing, electricity, and a stove — luxuries many families had never known. She immediately involved Nan, who had proved how much she knew about building things in her efforts at Val-Kill, putting her to work starting a crafts shop and a forge and helping design the interiors of the houses, with Eleanor often paying her out of her own pocket. The First Lady took others with her to

Arthurdale, enlisting the financial help of her great friend Bernard Baruch, who supported her despite FDR's growing impatience that not enough progress had been made to resist the howls of the Congress. Eleanor did not care about a congressman's objections. The image she saw of a child sheltering a pet rabbit so that it would not be eaten for supper never left her. A record of her travels to the West Virginia resettlement project alone was enough to show that she was unsparing in her own efforts to do everything she could. As soon as she was back in the White House, she began calling government offices to ask what they could do.

Meanwhile, Marion was struggling to keep an exclusive private girls' school in New York City going, and Nan was running the Democratic women's office in New York City and the furniture shop in Val-Kill. Both of them made time to go with Eleanor when they could. The roads that ran between Washington, New York, and Val-Kill were long and dark, and Eleanor traveled them without fear. Since the time she had met Clarence Pickett, executive secretary of the American Friends Service Committee, for her first visit to Arthurdale, she had seen the good that could be done by such organizations and the ways in which FDR's New Deal programs could help. When she met many of the families, she give them her heart, soon to be followed by her money and advocacy. For years she kept in touch with them, returning yearly to hand out diplomas to the high school graduates and inviting her Arthurdale friends to the White House. Arthurdale represented a forgotten world, and Eleanor would not stand by and do nothing. But the homestead projects, in West Virginia and elsewhere, began to attract more critics than friends.

•

There were some critics of Arthurdale within FDR's administration, especially Harold Ickes, FDR's secretary of the interior, and many in Congress thought the project was a waste of money. Public hearings and newspaper reports criticized the lack of progress in constructing houses. Indeed, Eleanor and Louis Howe made many mistakes in their rush to tackle the overwhelming needs: the first fifty houses were prefabricated and were inadequate for the site, it was difficult to get a safe water supply, and efforts to start factories failed. Despite all their efforts, very few jobs were created for former miners. In the end, the opposition was virile—the project was "communistic," Mrs. Roosevelt was a "publicity-seeker," and she was accused of promoting her own furniture industry at Val-Kill by linking it to the furniture industry Nan had started at Arthurdale. Hick regarded such charges as "Republican-inspired" and, as with other criticisms of the First Lady, she let the public outcry bother her more than it bothered Mrs. Roosevelt. All Eleanor had to do to regain her sense of optimism was to go to Arthurdale, visit in the homes where she knew the families, and be honored at receptions in the community center, where she enthusiastically took part in the square dancing. Often residents would meet her at the train station and give her a motorcade down the rutted roads to Arthurdale, where residents lined up on either side to wave to her. The children felt that she belonged to them. But congressional opposition won out, and in 1947 the last of the federal funds were cut off, and homes and community buildings were sold to private ownership.

The first Arthurdale homesteaders were the best advocates: from a hovel to a house was utopia. As one said, "We went to bed in hell and woke up in heaven." In 1947 they purchased their homes from the federal government and built a community for themselves around the schools and buildings. Despite the many bureaucratic failures and financial losses, Eleanor insisted that the proof of success was in the lives of families who for the first time had homes and land of their own. When she returned to Arthurdale, the families surrounded her with love as she asked about children by name, visited in their houses, and looked at their scrapbooks. "She was," one of the residents remembered, "the dearest woman I ever knew. She always thought about others."[2]

Today the past is preserved as Arthurdale Heritage, Inc., and the community is on the National Register of Historic Places. Many of the buildings have been restored, homeowners take pride in their houses, and staff and volunteers stage regular programs for visitors. One of the photographs on display shows Eleanor Roosevelt square dancing. Children thought the wife of the president of the United States visited every school and home.

The path from the White House to Arthurdale, West Virginia, ran through Val-Kill at Hyde Park, New York, where Eleanor and Nan first worked together to start a furniture factory to create jobs. In a stone cottage three women learned the importance of a home of their own. Her own rich background did not keep Eleanor from caring about how poor people lived; in fact, she seemed driven to know, and Marion and Nan, especially, cared too and struggled to keep up. No one seemed to have the energy of Eleanor Roosevelt, and once she went on the road to see for herself, there was no stopping her.

14

CHANGE COMES TO VAL-KILL

We kept house in the cottage, and Eleanor kept house in her cottage, and then we all were
over at the big house quite a bit, but we had ours separate. — Marion Dickerman

Eleanor's move to Washington, D.C., distanced her from Marion and Nan both physically and emotionally, but she also made choices for herself that distanced her even more. In 1932 she rented a third-floor walkup from Esther and Elizabeth at 20 East 11th Street in Greenwich Village. She would use it until 1945 as an escape from the White House, although she and Tommy took bags of correspondence to be answered while they were there. At the apartment Tommy typed Eleanor's first "My Day" newspaper column for daily syndication (31 December 1935), and it drew more than a thousand letters a week from her readers, most of them women. She invited Earl Miller and her brother, Hall—each increasingly restless—to use the apartment when either needed a place to stay in the city. Although it was a hideaway for Eleanor, the cozy new apartment with Tommy and Esther and Elizabeth nearby also competed with Val-Kill as a sanctuary.

By the summer of 1936 Eleanor was spending less and less time at Val-Kill and asking Nan to host Eleanor's family and friends in the guest room. Perhaps Eleanor never verbalized it, but Nan and Marion realized that she had shifted the focus of her life someplace else. Springwood was more welcoming now because Sara and her staff entertained presidential parties, and Sara recognized that Eleanor was essential to her son's success. FDR left Washington by special train for Hyde Park whenever he felt he could get away.[1] At his home in the Hudson Valley he experienced rest and happiness that he found nowhere else. Meetings with his White House advisers were more relaxed, and his staff had adapted themselves to working at Springwood. The locals had to contend with the guard stations on the Albany Post Road, but life at Hyde Park was not much disrupted for the president himself.

At Val-Kill, the energy had moved away from the cottage and outdoors to the crowded picnics. The comings and goings created problems for Marion and Nan, who lived in the path of it all. Eleanor often took her early morning walks on the trails alone because her frenetic schedule at the White House and her national travels left little personal time.

Eleanor was ready for a change, and in the summer of 1936 she proposed to Marion and Nan that they take the cottage and she would renovate the shop next door as a home for herself with an apartment for Tommy. Her proposal was not intended to end the friendship. "We kept house in the cottage, and Eleanor kept house in her cottage, and then we all were over at the big house quite a bit, but we had ours separate," Marion remembered. "That was terribly important from Nan's point of view and we loved it. We did many, many things together, but that was the way it worked out."[2] As they divided up their common property Eleanor wrote Nan and Marion, "What is mine is thine."[3] But the center had shifted.

As the shop renovations were nearing completion, Eleanor served notice of another change when she asked that Nan not move the furniture Otto Berge was making for her into her new home. Traditionally, she had depended on Nan to arrange her interiors. Now she wanted to direct where things would go: her books on the new bookshelves, photographs in her upstairs bedroom, a favorite chair and a bed on her sleeping porch. Along with her share of the linens and silver marked with the friends' initials, Eleanor took a domestic routine of work and play from Val-Kill to her new home. Tommy's suite of rooms on the first floor included an office where she and Eleanor worked and a living room where guests gathered for cocktails before dinner. (Eleanor herself did not drink, except an occasional glass of wine.) Marion and Nan were left to fill in the empty spaces in the cottage. They moved things around to suit themselves, but Eleanor's absence became more deeply experienced.

For a time, the two households existed side by side, less than two hundred feet apart, and Eleanor continued to invite Marion and Nan to picnics and parties. Marion and Nan watched from the margins the comings and goings of the Roosevelts' many guests—they were not yet outsiders, but no longer were they in the most intimate inner circle either. FDR and Eleanor felt free to use Val-Kill as a picnic site for entertaining official guests, with political discussions conducted at the swimming pool and over lunch. When the prospect of World War II began to ravage Europe, relations with America were intensified, and FDR's conversations with visiting dignitaries took on much greater significance. A picnic was no longer just a picnic: it was a time to solidify national interests. The fact that FDR found many of his women guests so charming added to the occasion. When Sara welcomed members of the royal families of England (the King and Queen of England visited in June 1939), the Netherlands, and Norway to Springwood, FDR also invited them to Val-Kill and to Top Cottage, which he had built uphill from Eleanor's house for his retirement years. Nan's new 16-millimeter camera recorded the famous people who swam in the pool in borrowed bathing suits Marion brought out from the bathhouse (she found one for Winston Churchill) and the women and men in formal dress who sat in the shade (among them Sara Delano Roosevelt, Queen Wilhelmina and her family, Queen Elizabeth and King George VI of England, Princess Martha and Crown Prince Olaf of Norway, and Frances Perkins, secretary of labor). Eleanor, Nan, and Marion dressed more formally now. It had been a decade since Eleanor had ordered knickers made like Nan's to wear on their camping trips and their travels around the state. Now they often wore white dresses for picnics, Eleanor sometimes balancing her pocketbook on one arm as she roasted a hot dog. Nan wore her white dresses into the woodworking shop. Change had come to Val-Kill in many ways.

The landscape had changed too, moving closer to a designed landscape that said "welcome." The bridge and roads were improved. FDR planted more trees, especially northern white cedars. In 1935 the old pool had been filled in. A modern new pool built by the terrace near the cottage became a focal point for entertaining. On their side, Marion and Nan added patios and garden furniture. It seemed that Nan in particular was determined to put her stamp on the place while all about her the Roosevelts' political cronies clamored for attention. One of the most pleasant additions was an orchard in the meadow across from the creek for raspberries, blueberries, grapes, apple and pear trees, and bee hives.

Nan added formal beds and enclosed porches and a loggia. She planted for seasonal color, using not only native plants but exotics as well. There were flowering shrubs, boxwoods, and vines of beautiful wisteria, clematis, and the heavenly blue morning glories that were Nan's favorites. Spirea, dogwood, mock oranges, and Eleanor's favorites — tea roses and bulbs, especially snowdrops — colored the landscape. Eleanor especially enjoyed the cutting garden, making her own small selections of flowers to bring into her house. She wanted a natural, low-maintenance landscape around her, and the garden reflected her wishes with seasonal bulbs and annuals planted by Charles Curnan, who worked for the Roosevelts. In autumn Eleanor delighted in the goldenrods and black-eyed Susans that grew along the roadside. The rough natural setting that had been the private picnic spot for Franklin, Eleanor, and Nan became nothing fancy and yet, perhaps, the most famous political playground in America. A personal vision of three women and Franklin to give the women a place to relax had lasting consequences.

15

DRIFTING APART AND A TRAGIC TALK

I am glad to have been honest at last. — Eleanor Roosevelt

Eleanor's decision to withdraw from Val-Kill Industries in May 1936 had caused a major disruption in the friends' relationship and ended the continuation of the business. She and her family and friends had accounted for many of the purchases, and she was responsible for most of the marketing. Her orders, her receptions at the Roosevelt house in New York on East 65th Street to show off the furniture, her appearances at department store sales, and her name on brochures and in news stories carried the enterprise. But Marion and Nan had reason to resent the fact that news reporters gave credit for the business to Eleanor Roosevelt. Nan bore the stress of running the business, and with her Democratic Party work and travel back and forth to Arthurdale, she was worn out. Val-Kill Industries had been a point of great pride for the women; now it was a problem to be dealt with, although Eleanor avoided keeping Nan and Marion up-to-date about her changing priorities.

Eleanor handled the change badly, publicly announcing the closing in a one-page press release: "Miss Nancy Cook, President of Val-Kill, who has conducted the shop since its founding, finds the various crafts projects have grown to such an extent that she can no longer give them her personal attention."[1] Otto Berge would take over the machinery for his own shop, and Nelly Johannesen, the weaving. Eleanor and Nan were interested in trying to help the people who had worked for them start their own businesses and gave them equipment to make that possible. Marion and Nan knew that Eleanor's interest had waned and that problems with the shop had increased: there were fewer orders and less respect for Nan's authority in Eleanor's absence. But Eleanor's announcement was nevertheless a shock. Listening to

Marion talk about it, historian Kenneth Davis gave it his own interpretation: "The dry, matter-of-fact words told nothing of the heartache this meant to Nancy Cook, who had invented this enterprise and for whom it had been the center, the essence of creative self-expression."[2]

In the summer of 1936, as Eleanor took steps to close down the shop the following year, she also began to step back from her commitment to Todhunter. Tensions mounted between her and Marion and Nan. Friends who become business partners often find that their friendship suffers, but apparently the three women had not anticipated any problems. "When it became necessary for us to give up the Val-Kill Industries," Marion said, "Eleanor took over the shop and made it a home of her own. This was understood and accepted for she wished to entertain more than had been possible at the cottage. Ownership at first did not become a vital point."[3] Yet it seemed they could no longer agree on anything. They disagreed about how to divide up what they had so happily owned jointly, including a school fund into which they had put profits. Franklin was invited to weigh in, and he apparently reassured each of the women that she was right (a notable FDR characteristic). Marion explained years later, "See, our arrangement was with Franklin when he gave us the land, that it belonged to the three of us."

Eleanor and Tommy were staying in the renovated house next door when Tommy wrote Eleanor's daughter, Anna, that Marion and Nan, deeply unhappy with the loss of their closeness to Eleanor, had been rude to her. Perhaps they did not say so, but they had lost her not just to new friends but to a huge American audience: in 1938 *Time* magazine had named Eleanor Roosevelt the greatest living American woman. In addition to the separation of their households, Nan had lost the furniture factory and Marion had lost Eleanor's partnership at Todhunter. Life on the Val-Kill had begun in tenderness, and Eleanor had evolved in that supportive environment; now she was ready to declare her personal independence. In describing Eleanor's refusal to meet with her to talk things over, Marion said, "She could be very hard, and sometimes cruel."[4] When Eleanor had refused to accept Val-Kill Industries picture frames that she thought were faulty, Nan said she was unkind. What had happened to the "Three Graces" who had loved one another for more than fifteen years?

Eleanor became more attentive to the needs of her grown children and her grandchildren, and their needs began to define Val-Kill—the pool with a diving board, a large fieldstone fireplace for outdoor cooking, the lawns, the swing set and seesaw for the grandchildren, who adored their grandmother. They liked to swim, they enjoyed the picnics and afternoon teas on the lawn, and they sat and listened while Grandmère read to them from Kipling's *Just So Stories*. The Roosevelts—as the Kennedys would be a generation later—were a large, active, and boisterous lot, and the grandchildren got along well together. The granddaughters thought of Marion and Nan as affectionate "great-aunts." Eleanor's granddaughter Nina remembers that Grandmère always had a varied group of friends. "Val-Kill was a place of complete acceptance."[5] (Eleanor's sons and grandsons cultivated Franklin's attention but were not as admiring of Eleanor's friends as her daughter Anna and her granddaughters were.) Nina helps account for the feeling both family and friends had: "My mother said you always felt that you were the most important person in the world to Eleanor Roosevelt."[6] Marion and Nan had felt that way for a long time, but after a decade of having Eleanor much to themselves, they felt pushed out.

Eleanor's big family now had the run of the place. Grandchildren trampled on Nan's gardens, and Marion's dog, Dean, bit visitors. The three women disagreed about keeping the leaves raked and paying the bills. The divine peace was like a balloon floating farther and farther away, until one day Marion and Nan looked up and it was gone.

A tragic disagreement among the three friends came to a head over the summer of 1938. On 28 June Marion left Nan behind in the cottage to spend the better part of the summer as one of a nine-member American presidential commission sent to study industrial relations in Britain and Sweden. Eleanor celebrated Marion's appointment by sending flowers and a check to her cabin. Tommy commented that Marion's trip abroad "leaves Nan high and dry and very lonesome and forlorn looking."[7] While Marion was away, the delicate balance in the three women's relationship was shattered during a heart-to-heart talk in the cottage between Eleanor and Nan. Nan was lonely and unprotected by Marion. Eleanor was not a vindictive person, and yet something transpired in that conversation that hurt her so badly that she struck back.

Marion recounted in an interview more than thirty years later that when she returned from Europe on 18 August 1938, Nan met her at the dock in near hysterics, her eyes red from weeping. Marion was stunned by the way Nan looked. Biographer Blanche Wiesen Cook believes that Nan had been drinking to assuage her loneliness. If Nan told Marion the cause of her tears, Marion did not report it in her interview with Kenneth Davis. All Nan was able to say at the time was that she and Eleanor "had a tragic talk during which things were said which never should have been said."[8] In an exchange of letters (retained by both women in their papers) we learn from Eleanor what it was.

•

For some context: Eleanor had spent most of the summer of 1938 at Hyde Park. Earlier in the year she had confessed to Lorena Hickok that she was "pulling myself back in all my contacts now."[9] Hick knew what that felt like: after the first intense years, Eleanor had changed the terms of their relationship as well, finally admitting that she no longer wanted an exclusive relationship with Hick. Although Eleanor always tried to keep her nearby, she had added many other friends to her circle, especially young people. Among the most important of these was thirty-year-old liberal activist Joseph Lash, who had introduced her to the American Youth Congress (AYC).

In August 1938 the AYC was meeting with the World Congress at Vassar College in Poughkeepsie, and some of the delegates came early to Val-Kill to talk with Mrs. Roosevelt. Eleanor was so enthusiastic about meeting with them that she had given up her chance to join FDR in Canada. The prospect of seeing some of the seven hundred young people from foreign countries whose advocacy for peace she believed was the most imperative need in the world excited her tremendously. The AYC was not an interest that Eleanor shared with Marion and Nan. In fact, Marion did not like the group at all, and she thought the young people merely flattered Eleanor. Moreover, she thought Eleanor should have been offended by their rude behavior.

Earl Miller, constant in his attentions and always available when Eleanor needed him, was sometimes at Val-Kill, too. After long days of hearing the AYC presentations at Vassar, Eleanor returned in the evening to spend time with Earl, whom Marion tolerated at best because they were old friends and he seemed to make Eleanor happy. The twelve-year age difference between the two did not seem to matter to either of them. Eleanor rushed from the students at Vassar home to her cottage to see Earl.

At about this time Eleanor wrote Hick that things were not going happily on the Val-Kill. Nan seemed forlorn and complained that she had not seen enough of her. Life had gotten too complicated. Eleanor wanted to simplify her relationships. She explained in an August letter to her daughter, Anna:

> I've been a bit upset over Nan and her attitude here and after
> I got back [from visiting Hick on Long Island] a little thing
> precipitated a scene; so today I went over and had a calm talk
> explaining why my feeling had changed toward them both and
> that we must have a business like arrangement. I added that we
> could have a friendly, agreeable relationship but my old trust and
> respect was gone and could not be recovered and I thought they
> probably felt the same way and were quite certainly as justified
> as I was. I told her to tell Marion of our talk and now I await
> the latter's return on the 18th.... I am glad to have been honest
> at last.[10]

This letter to Anna raises an important question: why was Eleanor's old trust and respect in Marion and Nan gone? Although Eleanor eventually explained to Marion what she had found offensive in her conversation with Nan that August evening before Marion's return, she never said what had led up to her change of heart. She told Anna that Nan's "attitude" was causing problems at Val-Kill. Eleanor had always defended Nan's management of the Democratic Women's office when others complained, but perhaps now workers in the Val-Kill shop were complaining that they found her hard to get along with — she required that they follow her specific directions and fill out time sheets, and she made them redo work when she found it inferior. The workmen had begun to have their own pride in the shop. Eleanor recognized that her many guests were an intrusion on Marion and Nan's life, but she ignored the complications, an ingrained habit in the Roosevelt household.

Tommy reported to Anna and to Esther and Elizabeth that Nan sometimes refused to speak. By that time Eleanor had made an apartment for Tommy in her house, and Tommy had become her closest companion — as much friend as secretary. They worked long hours, traveled together, and lived under the same roof. (Even when Tommy had her own apartment in Washington, she spent most of her time in the White House.) For her part, Tommy was willing to do anything for Mrs. R. Tommy was tireless, witty, candid, undemanding, and totally loyal. At various times she wrote to Esther and Elizabeth, with whom she felt a special closeness, wishing that Mrs. R would not travel so much and that she would invite fewer guests home and be less generous to those who asked for favors, but Tommy was just letting off steam when life got so complicated. Mrs. R could do whatever suited her needs, and Tommy would back her up.

Perhaps Nan's "attitude" was her jealousy, her possessiveness? But loss of trust and respect? It is impossible to know the answer to that question. If Eleanor was looking for reasons to change her living arrangement at Val-Kill, she found them.

If what Eleanor described to Anna as a "calm talk" was what left Nan in tears, Eleanor had badly misjudged Nan's response at the time. Months later Eleanor wrote a series of letters to Marion that laid out her grievances. The long typed letters were detailed, stern, and litigious. They reveal a different side of Eleanor, a woman relentlessly arguing in her own defense. She did not flinch from saying harsh things—a dramatic demonstration of how far she had come from the days of submitting to her mother-in-law. It had taken a long time for Eleanor to recognize that she no longer trusted Marion and Nan, but when she did, she said so in no uncertain terms. It didn't matter what they or other friends might say about her. She now stood up for herself. During her White House years, when critics wrote vicious things about her, she was mostly successful in ignoring them. As she once said to Lorena Hickok when gossips talked about them, "I care so little what 'they' say."[11] During the Val-Kill years, put to the test when she felt insulted by friends, Eleanor had become a tough and determined woman.

This imperfect interregnum lasted from 1936 to 1938, a time when Marion and Nan lived a few hundred yards from Eleanor, and although Eleanor continued to invite them to family occasions and Nan continued to be in charge of picnics, they were wary of setting off a new round of disagreements—whether over raking the leaves, or leashing the dogs, or paying the bills. Anger and hurt were so mixed up in each of them that making peace seemed to require more energy than anyone had left to give. These were years in which a dark cloud settled over the paradise that had been Val-Kill, and nothing was ever going to be the same.

16

AN EXCHANGE OF LETTERS

I am unable to live a life based on an illusion. — Eleanor Roosevelt

The summer of 1938 lay like a stone in the hearts of Eleanor, Marion, and Nan, and what had been times of pleasure on the banks of the Val-Kill became awkward moments of avoiding one another. Tommy and Eleanor returned to Washington in the fall, and Eleanor threw herself into a round of meetings and travel, but she could no longer ignore what was bothering her. One weekend in October when she and Tommy had escaped the White House to spend a few days in her apartment in the Greenwich Village brownstone owned by Esther and Elizabeth, she took to her bed. Tommy was so upset that she called Esther and Elizabeth to tell them that Eleanor had "turned her face to the wall" and would not speak. She had descended into one of her black moods. Even Franklin was so concerned that he was making no other appointments, waiting to hear that Eleanor was well again. Esther said that Tommy's call had driven them to "despair."[1] Esther and Elizabeth had seen Eleanor in one of her dark moods before, but this was unexpected. In a few days Eleanor appeared at their apartment to explain her behavior. Years later, Esther reported what Eleanor had said: "I know it is your dinner time and I have guests waiting, but there is something I must tell you. I know you think I have been very ill. I have not. You know I have always been aware that people anxious to gain my interest were really hoping thereby for a link with Franklin. I have known this but there is one person of whom this did not seem to me to be true. Don't ask how I could make such a fundamental error. I simply did. I have recovered from my disappointment. That, after all, is based on my own weakness.... I simply had to let you know that all is now well. I am unable to lead a life based on an illusion."[2] Eleanor had always been able to talk to Esther and Elizabeth, who were good listeners, intelligent and stable women, and utterly devoted to her. "I am overcome now and then by the shameless way in which I tell you all the little things of life," she wrote to Esther, "but then they do make up the major part of our existence, don't they?"[3] A burden had been shared, and Eleanor was ready to confront Marion and Nan.

A letter from Eleanor to Marion and Nan, written on White House stationery, laid out her version of their history. In it, she reveals how something Nan had said the evening of their talk cut her to the quick.

> If you will look back, I think you will realize that in all of our relationship I have never before wanted anything, nor suggested anything about the cottage or the school, and therefore it is entirely natural that we have had no difficulties in previous years. This was quite easy for me because I had no objection to acceding to your wishes. . . .
>
> I have decided to turn over to you now, instead of at my death, my entire interest in the cottage, the shop building and the other buildings, exclusive of the stable which was built entirely with my money. . . .
>
> I shall, of course, take everything out of the building which I have paid for and store it until I build somewhere else. If I had had any idea of how you both felt when I planned the remodeling of the building [how they felt we do not know], I would never have spent the many thousands of dollars which I have spent. . . .
>
> This has been a very costly lesson both financially and spiritually, but it is good for me to know that one can never know how any other person reasons or what motivates them.

All of her life Eleanor had borne hurt in silence by turning inward. Now she minced no words, although she had not yet clearly explained the cause of her hurt. She returned to the business of breaking up her association with Todhunter:

> In view of what has happened I feel that I wish also to withdraw entirely from the school. I will give you both with great pleasure

my share of the school fund which has been held in my name
and on which I have paid income tax every year. I do not expect
you to take my name off the letter head this year if that will cause
you any embarrassment. I am sure however, that you will prosper
better without any connection with the name.

I shall only come to Hyde Park when the President is at the big
house and I will stay at the big house.[4]

In a letter written to Marion a few weeks later she came to the heart
of the matter:

[Nan] told me, for instance, that while we were working in the
[Women's Democratic] committee, in the school, and in the
industries together, you had both always felt that whatever was
done was done for the sole purpose of building me up. My whole
conception was entirely different. I went into the industries
because I felt that Nan was fulfilling something which she had
long wanted to do. I would never have done it alone. I had neither
the knowledge nor the background nor the interest.

I went into the school because I had an interest in education
and in young people and being fond of you I was anxious to
help you in what you wanted to do. It gave me an opportunity
for regular work which I was anxious to have. I went into
the political work because Louis was anxious to have me do
something to keep up Franklin's interest in a field which he
eventually hoped Franklin would return to. I had no personal
ambitions of any kind and I have none today.[5]

It was disingenuous for the best-known American woman in public life to insist that she had no personal ambition and to fall back on
her frequently stated wish to help others. One more revealing phrase,
however, does leap out: Eleanor was insulted by Nan's having said
that she and Marion were in partnership with her "for the sole purpose of building me up." Eleanor knew how hard she had worked to

get where she was. And she knew how much she had loved Nan and Marion and felt loved by them. It was a poisonous phrase.

Marion was temperate in her response: "First I was no part of your talk & Nan's last summer and feel that I should be allowed to speak for myself. I do not know where this 'building up' idea came from. . . . I have never used the expression nor entertained the idea. . . . Unless you wish to refer to this matter again I shall consider it closed for I have found nothing in it but disillusionment and unhappiness."[6]

In a letter to Hick at the end of the summer, Eleanor revealed another aspect of her quarrel with Marion that she had brought up in her "tragic talk" in the cottage with Nan. Eleanor was hosting a picnic for one hundred guests when, unknown to her, her brother Hall showed up—drunk again. He went over to sit on the patio with Nan and Marion, who gave him a drink, probably more than one. When he returned to the picnic he was in a reckless mood and tossed his son, Danny, into the air. He lost control and dropped the boy, who fell to the ground, injured. It was agreed that he needed to be driven immediately to the hospital. Hall got behind the wheel of his car, and Marion got in with Danny. As they were leaving, Hall drove into a ditch; a state trooper had to drive them to the hospital. After they arrived and Danny was being treated for a broken collarbone, Marion called to tell Eleanor what had happened. Eleanor erupted in a storm of accusations directed at Marion, who she insisted must have driven the car. Although Marion protested her innocence, Eleanor would not hear anything further. When they arrived back at Val-Kill and Marion went to her room, distraught, FDR sent her a note saying that he knew she had not been the driver and she should not blame herself. All of this came to light only in May 1939 when Marion chose to tell the story after Eleanor had initiated her earlier letters. Marion wrote:

Since I returned [from the 1938 trip to Europe] I have never had a chance to talk to you about anything. The only instance in which I am conscious of having displeased you was on the night I went to the hospital with Danny. My judgment in that instance may not have been wise. My motive however was a kindly one. I have never understood why you spoke to me that night as you did.... Three times I asked to see you in order to talk matters over. Each time you refused. I know nothing of what has brought this on my head save the incident to which I refer, [which] unless far more was implicated than I know of, seems rather out of proportion to all that went before.[7]

Marion thought Eleanor had overreacted. Eleanor responded that Marion should have let her know that Hall was drinking. Once more she referred to her "long and illuminating talk with Nan." Marion denied having been a part of the conversation. Suddenly, Marion and Nan were crossed up in their friendship with Eleanor. Perhaps this was an exception; at least, we have found no other evidence of a disagreement between Marion and Nan.

Even these exchanges do not fully explain the complexities of the impasse they had gotten themselves into, however, and there is a missing piece to the puzzle concerning Marion, as we shall see in the next chapter, that no other biographer has considered: the first discovered example of a rift between Marion and Nan, in which, it would seem, the balance between the two women may have been upended when Marion tipped the scales further toward FDR, with the help of a new friend, and Nan was left out in the cold. It is mere conjecture to suppose that Marion realized that she had not looked after Nan, as Eleanor always said she must, and that this failure gave Marion a reason to try to make up for it—realizing her mistake, being more protective of Nan, and intensifying her disagreements with Eleanor. It is an example in which jealousy may have come between them all, and although observers recognized that Eleanor's friends were a jealous lot, biographers have not found evidence that Marion and Nan were ever separated in their relations with Eleanor.

17

MISSING EVIDENCE

[Marion] did want to have some attention paid to her. — Frances Perkins

A long oral history interview with Frances Perkins, FDR's four-term secretary of labor, yields unexamined information about the weekend when Nan and Eleanor had their tragic talk and reveals buried details about Marion's absence from the cottage when it occurred.[1]

Perkins had an incisive mind, and she saw her associates often and at close hand. She understood Franklin and Eleanor Roosevelt in ways that perhaps could be best described by a woman of controlled emotional detachment and intellectual toughness. Perkins appreciated the close relationship Eleanor and Franklin forged for the good of the country, and she also knew they respected each other. She often depended on Mrs. Roosevelt to help present government recommendations to FDR and was especially appreciative of Eleanor's efforts to give her and Franklin private time together in Albany or Hyde Park so that she could have his close attention. She was less perceptive and generous in understanding Eleanor's friendship with Marion and Nan. Perkins had made it in a man's world (she was the first female cabinet secretary), and that may explain why she was dismissive of the importance of Val-Kill in Eleanor's life.[2]

Perkins recalled a time at the New York governor's mansion in Albany when Eleanor had told her that she did not mind sharing her room overnight with her because it wasn't really her home; in fact, she had never had a home of her own (the intimacy of the confession, which Eleanor later included in her autobiography, embarrassed Perkins). Then Perkins observed: "Of course, she had sometime or other fixed up that little Val-Kill cottage over by the swimming pool on the grounds that it was theoretically to be a house which she, Nancy Cook and Marion Dickerman had together. Nancy was to run the Val Kill factory and live over there, but the property, I think, stood in Mrs. Roosevelt's name. Anyhow, she had a part in it. It was a very informal affair, all finished off with rough boards. But it was hers." Perkins perhaps was confusing Stone Cottage with the renovated furniture factory with knotty pine walls, which Nan helped Eleanor achieve and which Eleanor so admired. At any rate, Perkins's taste ran to something more formal.

Perkins (living apart from her husband), with her daughter Susanna, shared a beautiful Georgetown house with the wealthy widow Mary Harriman Rumsey. After Rumsey died, Perkins made her Washington home with Caroline O'Day, another wealthy widow and a New York congresswoman, who was also a close friend of Marion Dickerman. Caroline, the widow of Daniel T. O'Day, heir to a Standard Oil fortune, was fifty years old and had grown children and a house of her own in Rye, New York. Because Perkins was so guarded, we cannot really know what role women played in her private life. More important for our purpose is that Perkins's interview includes missing pieces of the puzzle of what happened after Marion returned home.

For weeks Marion had lobbied Franklin to be included in the American commission studying industrial relations in Britain and Sweden. She had talked it over with FDR's close adviser, Bernard Baruch, who had taken on Marion as one of the women he felt needed looking after, especially in managing their business interests. On hearing of Marion's desire to be on the commission, he urged FDR to send her. FDR was persuaded and told Perkins to include her. Perkins was incredulous, arguing that Marion was little more than an ordinary schoolteacher and did not deserve to be in the group. In fact, Marion had been studying American labor issues, especially as they affected women, for most of her adult life, though at a lower level certainly than Perkins. FDR finally insisted that Perkins would just have to include her. Although she thought it was an absurd idea, Perkins did. Already in Europe herself, Perkins cabled Marion that she was on the commission, and Marion began at once to get her travel plans in order. Perhaps Perkins had never before expressed her anger at having been forced to make such an unsuitable choice—not to FDR or to anyone else—and when she said so in the interview years later, she really let her hair down.

At some length Perkins demeaned Marion's qualifications to be a delegate, and then she described in detail Marion's flamboyant behavior once she got to Europe. Anna Rosenberg, a prominent New York businesswoman, political insider, and the only other woman on the commission, had taken Marion in hand and encouraged her to have a good time. Anna was hard to ignore—she was "quick as a cat and plenty smart"—and she had made herself useful to FDR and would do the same with later presidents. Anna took Marion to the best shops, and Marion bought a new dress. Marion had her hair done, flirted with the men, danced, and generally, Perkins said, made a fool of herself. It was a cruel depiction of Marion as a spinster who "had always been stuck in a corner, who did want to be noticed, did want to have some attention paid to her. . . . It would boost her stock in her school, her standing in New York." Marion often asked for favors from those who could help her: she asked Eleanor to speak at many public occasions, for her own events and on behalf of others; she asked to attend White House affairs and to stay overnight; she asked to be given New York theater tickets; and she asked Eleanor for personal letters from Eleanor to Todhunter students and parents and to host her school groups and friends in Washington. Perkins, having negotiated politics all her adult life on her own merits, in Albany and then in Washington, must have found Marion's methods especially unacceptable.

In the week after they returned from Europe, Anna Rosenberg sent Marion copies of the commission's report and added a personal note that confirms Marion's willingness to ask for what she wanted: "I am also enclosing the wallet which you asked me to get for you. I hope you like it." The closing, "Cordially," was struck out, and Anna wrote "Love" instead.[3] In Europe, according to Perkins, Marion and Anna played while the other members of the study commission did the work. At night Anna rounded up two men whose wives were not with them and took them dancing with her and Marion. Perkins and some of the wives agreed that their behavior was outrageous, though no impropriety seems to have occurred. Aboard ship coming home, the men went to work to prepare a report to hand in to President Roosevelt as soon as they returned; one of them went to his own New York office on Sunday to meet his secretary to prepare a finished document. Before disembarking, Anna asked for and received a copy of the rough draft.

We then learn from the Perkins interview a vital missing piece in Marion's story of what happened next: at some point before the ship docked in New York on 18 August, Marion had invited Anna to come home with her to stay in the Val-Kill cottage, and Anna had accepted. When Nan met the ship in New York, Marion, accompanied by the dashing Anna Rosenberg, was in high spirits—she had never had such a time! Exactly what transpired at the reunion on the dock is unknown. While Anna and Marion gathered all their European baggage to transport to the cottage, did Marion, ignoring Nan's overwrought condition, whisper to her to please hurry ahead and get things ready in the guest room? It seems likely. Certainly it was something Nan often did when Eleanor had unexpected guests. And then off they went to Val-Kill, where Marion showed off the cottage—and its proximity to Springwood—to Anna.

When Marion discovered that FDR was at Springwood, she immediately asked Eleanor to take her and Anna to see him in order to give him a firsthand report of the commission's work. When they met with the president, Marion gave all the credit for the work to Anna and regaled Franklin with stories of the adventure, the details he was eager to hear. He, as Frances knew, loved gossip. They talked and he laughed. When a commission member tried to set up a meeting after the president had returned to Washington, FDR said there was no need—he already had the report. Frances cautioned him that he had better soft-pedal that news and give credit to the commission for the work.

And that was that, although what the commission actually accomplished is missing from Perkins's interview, and apparently from FDR's interests. He took no action on the report when it was finally sent to him as the handiwork of the commission.

It was a setup for a perfect storm: Marion's high spirits when she returned to the States with Anna, Nan's near hysteria after her talk with Eleanor, Marion's immediate defection from the cottage to take Anna to see FDR at Springwood. And the next day, Marion had to pick up the pieces and defend Nan. She left no record of thoughts on how her own neglect may have affected her partner's feelings. Both Nan and Eleanor had said more than they meant to in their talk. Perhaps Marion was feeling guilty about her grand holiday without Nan. Marion and Nan had weathered other storms, and they would not let this one weaken their partnership. The fragile relationship of E M N, however, was about to succumb to forces of human nature.

Perhaps only a philosopher such as Pascal provides an insight missing in the discussion (words known to Eleanor, fluent in French): *Le cœur a ses raisons, que la raison ne connaît point.*

18

AFTER THE STORM

Bless you and all my love. — Nan

Before lawyers in 1938 finally drafted the Val-Kill legal settlement to dissolve the partnership, softening qualities in Eleanor, Marion, and Nan returned to the fore. A letter to Eleanor from Nan, written after Eleanor had moved out of the cottage and was living next door, began by using Eleanor's sons' nickname for her.

> Dear Muddie:
> This is just a reminder for you to look up and see if you have a free day. It could be on Wednesday or Thursday, which would probably be better for you, sometime the latter part of May or the first of June, for the Annual State Meeting of the Women's Division.
> It was nice seeing you at Hyde Park, and it looks as though this weather was going to keep up. Marion hopes to get to Hyde Park this weekend. She hasn't been up for a long time.
> I ordered the seeds for the herbs, and Clifford will plant them in my new hot box, so I am in hopes that you and Tommy will have good seasoning for your soups next summer. Too bad I can't raise the beef in the hot box also....
> Bless you and all my love.[1]

In her own handwriting Nan added, "with a kiss." Eleanor appended a handwritten note at the bottom of Nan's letter for Tommy to let Nan know she could come June first or second.

Then after many months of silences and delays, a legal agreement was drawn up in November in which Eleanor bought out Marion's and Nan's interest in the cottage and paid them for what they had invested in the shop building she was about to own outright to turn into her home. They gave up investments they had made in the shop and agreed to give the equipment to employees, who would open businesses at other sites. Eleanor's friends, informed by Tommy about the proceedings, considered that she had been too generous, especially in turning over the Todhunter School fund that had accumulated modest profits, but she insisted that she wanted to ease Marion's and Nan's fear about their future if she could. The financial settlement was complicated, and who had paid for what is inexact, but a price tag could not be put on Marion's and Nan's greatest investment: making a new life possible for Eleanor. Nan had been a tireless worker in the shop and the gardens, and she and Marion had hosted countless picnics for Eleanor and FDR. There had not been a lot of money made and lost. It had not been a costly experiment despite the failure of the furniture industry. As First Lady Eleanor began making significant money writing and lecturing (and advertising consumer products on her radio program), and generous by nature, she could afford to be generous now.

The years of the breakup also came at a very difficult time: Nan had unspecified health problems, or maybe she was tired and feeling old.[2] There was so much for Eleanor to worry about privately: the children's hasty marriages and divorces. But World War II cast the darkest shadow over America, and it was on everybody's mind, especially FDR and his cabinet as he contemplated the buildup to the war from 1939 until America's entry in 1941. Eleanor was alarmed that at home New Deal programs and social justice issues were being forgotten. During the worst of the Depression years Americans by the thousands had written letters to Mrs. Roosevelt asking for her help.

Then on Sunday, 7 December 1941, "the day that shall live in infamy," the Japanese bombing of American ships docked at Pearl Harbor gave the president and the Congress the reason to declare war and the country reason to give up isolationism. Eleanor was entertaining guests at a large luncheon at the White House and did not hear the news—from one of the ushers—until midafternoon. Only after Franklin had finished meetings with his military advisers and congressional leaders did Eleanor have a chance to visit with him privately in his room. She found him "more serene" now that the decision to go to war had been made.[3] Apparently Marion and Nan were in the cottage at Val-Kill, desperately out of touch with Eleanor and Franklin. Friends who are separated in times of national peril often feel especially frightened. This news must have intensified their need to speak with their old friends.

When America entered World War II, Eleanor's correspondence shifted to letters from desperate women asking for news of their sons, husbands, and boyfriends. Eleanor traveled to the South Pacific to see American women and men in uniform, included Jose Lash, and returned home to contact families of those she had seen in hospitals. At home she helped publicize war bonds and other ways for ordinary citizens to support the war. Her work took her far from Hyde Park, where her visits were infrequent, and then she kept company with Franklin when he tried to get away for some rest at Springwood. It was not a time for Eleanor to see Marion and Nan, who were dealing with their own problems—Nan's health and Marion's difficulties at trying to keep Todhunter operating. They had their own efforts for America. A victory garden at Val-Kill was but a small way of supporting the war effort (and Eleanor had a White House Victory Garden). Marion continued to attend labor relations conferences in Washington, D.C. For Eleanor, trying to work her way through her personal difficulties with Marion and Nan on top of everything else was asking a lot. But they all tried, and time was not on their side.

Memories of many years of happiness and achievement could not be erased. How could the women move past the bitter disappointments? Marion and Nan were family. Forgiveness is not easily come by in a family quarrel; things are best left unsaid. Unfortunately, all three of them began to talk about their troubles, although what more was said remains shrouded in shadows.

Before Thanksgiving in 1938 Eleanor announced curtly that, having signed the final agreement, she was moving ahead and would be installing a new furnace in the cottage. She suggested that Otto Berge be allowed to take the remaining lumber in the cellar. Loose ends were tied up; exchanges continued. In January 1940 Eleanor was not able to accommodate Marion and Nan for more than one night at the White House for the Conference on Children, nor could she make a place for them at the dinner, which had been reduced to twenty-two, mostly officials who had to be included. She observed that there were many people attending the meetings who wanted to meet with her. FDR's attention was riveted to the war news, and the White House was no longer a place to have a good time. A few weeks later Eleanor wrote Marion to explain that she was not inviting the usual people to FDR's considerably changed birthday party January 30; there would be no stunts or speeches or gifts. In February, however, Eleanor made arrangements for the Todhunter girls to spend a week in the White House when Marion brought them to Washington. Then in May Eleanor declined to give the Todhunter commencement speech, refusing all year-end invitations except the one from Arthurdale.

The year 1941 was tumultuous personally for the Roosevelts: after a period of declining health, Sara Delano Roosevelt died on 7 September. Hours later a huge oak suddenly crashed to the ground in front of Springwood; Franklin sat on the lawn and grieved to himself. Days later when he was going through some of his mother's papers he discovered that she had saved in an envelope some of his boyhood curls, and he asked to be alone, to weep. Eleanor confessed that she felt "no deep affection or sense of loss."[4] On the same day she had sat by the bedside watching the slow and agonizing death of her brother, Hall, who had been like a son to her and whose brilliance had been dissipated in a life of alcohol. How had she failed to save him? It was a question the family had asked about her own father, also dead from alcoholism. She plunged deeper into work, putting America's needs first, a salve for her soul. The year turned outward toward the battlefields.

From America's entry into the war in December 1941 until the war ended in September 1945, Eleanor asked what she could do as a mother, not only to support her own four sons who now were in uniform (and Anna's husband John Boettiger) but also to reach out to other families in her travels. Although life always goes on, there is no question but that, as Eleanor, Marion, and Nan struggled to resolve their personal differences, the public lives of President and Mrs. Roosevelt were all-consuming. The compelling news shifted away from the domestic front to overseas, and FDR was absorbed in trying to chart a course for America, the history of which has been told many times. What it meant on a personal level for Eleanor, Marion, and Nan was that a quiet life on the Val-Kill had been made all the more impossible by world events.

But an event that shook the world was President Roosevelt's death 12 April 1945. Although he had returned from Yalta looking gravely ill, Eleanor and his family hoped that he would revive by going immediately to rest at Warm Springs. Eleanor remained in Washington, going on with a meeting as she had promised. In Warm Springs, unknown to Eleanor, Franklin had a special guest, Lucy Mercer Rutherfurd (Winthrop Rutherfurd had died in 1944). Lucy had brought artist Madam Elizabeth Shoumatoff to Warm Springs to paint FDR's portrait. Other guests included his cousins Laura Delano and Margaret Suckley and his secretary, Grace Tully. Henry Morgenthau Jr. had been at dinner with them the evening before. But even the sight of old friends did not restore him to health. He was stricken with a cerebral hemorrhage and died almost immediately. Eleanor was called back to the White House to receive the news she feared, and to notify the children, before flying to Warm Springs. There she received the news that Lucy had been with him at the time of his death. It was another broken promise, aided by their daughter Anna, but Eleanor seemed to draw from some deep well of inner resolve and would forgive Anna and recover her will to serve, though not immediately. At first she had to deal with family problems. After Franklin's death, Elliott Roosevelt moved to Top Cottage, evicted Moses Smith as his father's tenant (which Marion described as "a heartbreaking performance"), and began selling off properties. Elliott and his mother started a farming operation together and built a "tremendous chicken house," but they were never successful in any business. Eleanor always felt "a special solicitude for Elliott" and expected that Marion and Nan would accept the new arrangement. "This was not possible," Marion remembered.[5] The sanctity of Val-Kill had been destroyed for them—Marion and Nan knew that they could not stay. But it was not easy to pull up stakes and move away after some nineteen years of living at Val-Kill. Furthermore, they couldn't discuss the separation—it was "too charged with emotion"—and they had the president's lawyer work out the arrangements. There were so many distractions as the Roosevelt children decided what they wanted to do with the properties, and Marion and Nan were no part of the discussions. They had to stay in their cottage and wait to be told what was going to happen.

Marion and Nan were at the cottage when funeral preparations were made for FDR's burial in his mother's rose garden, according to his wishes. The Roosevelts' longtime superintendent of the Hyde Park estate, William Plog, was assigned the responsibility of laying out the plot where the president was to be buried. When Marion went over to ask if there was anything she could do to help, he said, "Come with me and we'll pace out the place together." And it was done. The president's "own men" from Hyde Park, not the undertaker who came from Poughkeepsie, dug the grave.[6] The Roosevelt children and grandchildren hurried to Hyde Park to join the family, but there was little consensus about how they might help their mother. Elliott and his wife, Faye Emerson, were ready to move into Top Cottage, and Elliott wanted to make other changes that dramatically threatened to end Marion's and Nan's quiet life at Stone Cottage. After 1945 Marion and Nan realized they could no longer live at Val-Kill; the signed agreement that each of the three women could live there for the rest of their lives meant nothing when all around them the Roosevelt family was making changes. Soon after FDR's death, Eleanor turned over the Big House to the United States, in accordance with her husband's wishes. She made her home at Val-Kill and purchased additional land from the Roosevelt estate. Her son John and his family later lived in Stone Cottage, and her son Elliott and his wife moved to Top Cottage.

For two years after Franklin's death, uncertain about what to do, Marion and Nan remained in Stone Cottage. It was an awkward and hurtful time, each of them mourning the loss of the man who had been at the center of their lives and the nation's for so long and unable to suffer with Eleanor, who was surrounded by quarreling children. The Allies were poised to make the final assault to win the war that FDR had so long contemplated. There would be no more Fireside Chats, no announcement of the peace. FDR was dead.

Val-Kill was also changed. No one had realized how much they had depended on FDR to hold the world together. Eleanor quickly moved out of the White House and divided up family furnishings with the children. Nan was unwell; Marion needed to make a living for the two of them. Every day presented some new problem—trying to look after the cottage and property. Marion and Nan were desperate to move away from the center of such change and conflict. When Marion was hired to work at the Marine Museum in Mystic, Connecticut—present-day Mystic Seaport—she saw a way to support herself and Nan. They now decided to sell their interest in Val-Kill to Eleanor. On 2 October 1947 they moved to make their home in New Canaan, Connecticut, to begin a new stage of their lives. They left the keys to the cottage on the table with a note wishing Eleanor well, and they drove away from Val-Kill, in grief for what they were leaving behind and with grave uncertainty about starting over. Nan was sixty-three years old; Marion, fifty-seven. Where had the time gone? Suddenly, they were feeling old and turned out. Marion took charge—they bought an attractive house in New Canaan, and Nan made a new garden. The neighbors welcomed them, curious to hear about their Roosevelt connections. They talked freely of their admiration for FDR and the many family occasions they had attended. If we can believe the interviews Marion gave after Eleanor's and Nan's deaths, she said little about her work with Eleanor. Now she was celebrated as an "intimate" of the greatest American president. Surrounded by furnishings they had brought from Val-Kill, Marion and Nan made a remarkable recovery of their confidence and their determination to make a new life for themselves.

It had been a hasty departure. Although Marion indicated in a letter written in July 1947 to Henry Hackett, the Roosevelts' lawyer in Poughkeepsie, that she and Nan would like to be allowed eighteen to twenty-four months to leave Stone Cottage, in fact they were ready in October. They asked to be allowed to take with them the kitchen equipment they had purchased for themselves. For the new gardens Nan would make, they took garden implements, a picket fence, and shrubs and plants that had been given to them by their good friend Bernard Baruch; these included taxus, azaleas, euonymus, viburnum, various perennials, asparagus, raspberries, and strawberries. Nan abandoned dresses in favor of sturdy work pants, friends reported that she sometimes used colorful language when she pleased, and she spent hours working in her gardens in Connecticut and showing them off to friends and neighbors. She especially enjoyed comparing notes with other members of the New Canaan Garden Club.

Marion and Nan made a lovely home for themselves on Sunset Hill Road in New Canaan, filling it with their treasures: a portrait of FDR hung over a Val-Kill chest, Val-Kill pewter candlesticks and a bowl on top of the chest, and over the fireplace a marble plaque from the White House dining room. Marion became an important member of the staff at the Marine Museum, organizing educational activities and the first corps of volunteers and hostesses. She also led efforts to create the Junior Museum and wrote a number of publications about the founders of Mystic Seaport. She took special pride in suggesting that the museum acquire FDR's boat, the *Vireo*, and in raising the funds to bring it to the museum for permanent exhibition.

When Eleanor had renovated the shop next door and made it her home, she had not insisted that Marion and Nan move from the cottage, nor did she go far away when she left it. She made her home next door because she was part owner and because she loved Val-Kill, but perhaps she also did not want to go so far from Marion and Nan and risk not seeing them again. She only had to look out from her sleeping porch to see the cottage. After Marion's and Nan's move to Connecticut, Marion came back to Val-Kill from time to time, but Nan never did. Eleanor more often went to them, sometimes driving herself, sometimes driven from Val-Kill by "Tubby" Curnan, her chauffeur. Nan's health worsened after she broke her hip, and Marion began a long period of trying to look after her at home with some outside help. Eleanor came "as much as she could ... [but] it wasn't the same. It couldn't be the same." But still, Marion comforted herself to remember, "There was never any break threatening [the friendship]."[7] Eleanor continued giving generous gifts, including checks.

When the Roosevelt family gathered at Springwood for Christmas 1944, it was to be their last. Three of the sons—James, Franklin Jr., and John—were overseas on military assignments. Only Elliott and Anna's husband, John Boettiger, were home on leave. Two days later Eleanor wrote readers of her "My Day" column, "I try to remember what an old friend of my grandmother's used to say: 'Enjoy every minute you have with those you love, my dear, for no one can take joy that is past away from you. It will be there in our heart to live on when the dark days come.'"[8]

After FDR's death, Eleanor began to make another life for herself. Her closest personal relationship in the last years of her life was with David Gurewitsch, who became her doctor and friend in 1945, and the woman he married, Edna Perkel. In 1959 she bought a New York City brownstone on East 74th Street with the Gurewitsches and lived there until she died. Joe and Trude Lash and their son and David and Edna Gurewitsch and their daughters were frequent visitors on Val-Kill weekends. In both cases Eleanor first formed an intimate friendship with the man—Joe as a young American radical; David was her mature, cultured European travel companion—and when they married she loved their wives and children. There was a definite romantic overtone to Eleanor's feelings for David. She wrote him, "You know without my telling you that I love you as I love and have never loved anyone else."[9] Perhaps she had at last met the man she could love.

The fact that it was impossible to think of him as a potential husband freed her to express her own feelings. He loved Mrs. Roosevelt, but not in a romantic way. Eleanor's romance may have been, after all, with America.

•

As Eleanor began her work with the United Nations—she was chosen by President Truman to be an American representative—and traveled the world, sometimes with friends and grandchildren, she did not forget the joy of Val-Kill. Amidst all the changes and her greatly expanded role as First Lady of the World, as Truman called her, she took pains to stay in touch with her old friends. Now letters to Marion and Nan followed exchanges of gifts and occasional visits to New Canaan and Hyde Park. There are several dozen letters of this kind in the Eleanor Roosevelt Papers in the archives of the Franklin D. Roosevelt Presidential Library and Museum, mostly from the 1950s, some from Marion to Eleanor and many from Eleanor to Marion and Nan. Many of the letters were written in response to the ritual exchange of presents at birthdays, Easter, and Christmas. Marion's are handwritten; most of Eleanor's were typed by Tommy. In order not to miss a special date when she was traveling abroad, Eleanor sent cards and gifts ahead of the occasion. A sampling of these letters suggests the constancy of the women's efforts to stay in touch. When Marion and Nan moved out of the cottage, Marion was concerned about Nan's physical frailty, but within a few months Marion wrote to say, "Nan is improved." In the fall of 1951 Eleanor longed to see pictures of the new house and garden in New Canaan. She wrote to Nan on 6 January 1954, "Do let me know when you can come to lunch with me and ask Marion if she would care to come," wanting them to see her new apartment at 211 East 62nd Street. Nan quickly accepted. By December, however, Eleanor's letters expressed alarm about Nan, who has been in the hospital suffering from shingles and other physical weaknesses. Nan's health continued to concern Marion—"Nan has had a dreadful time"—and in the spring of 1956 Eleanor wrote to say that she was glad that "Nan can get out a little."

In the summer of 1957 Eleanor drove to see Marion and Nan in New Canaan; in the fall Marion took three New Canaan friends to have lunch with Eleanor at Val-Kill. They arranged another visit in February 1958. Marion wrote to Eleanor, "One of the results of being famous is that often your friends are alerted to your plans. The fact that you are speaking in Stamford on April 24th is a case in point. Nan and I do hope you will plan to have luncheon with us that day. I can easily pick you up in Stamford as I did before. It will mean so much to Nan to have a chance to visit with you—even for a little while. . . . Her morale is and has been wonderful." In April, having just seen the play *Sunrise at Campobello* in New Haven, Marion wrote Eleanor asking if there was any way that she could get tickets for the New York performance (Marion was willing to pay any price) so that she could give them to a high school student who had visited them at Val-Kill. Eleanor appended a note for Tommy: "See if you can get four matinee tickets for April 30th." In November Eleanor set up a luncheon at Hyde Park to talk with Marion, four of Marion's friends, and Esther Lape about a U.S. Senate campaign.

Nan's health continued to be up and down, and in May 1960 Eleanor returned to New Canaan. Marion reported on the quiet pleasures she had missed at Val-Kill, "The sun is warm and Nan and I have been sitting on the south terrace."

Finally, after seeking Eleanor's advice in telephone calls and letters about Nan's various hospital stays and difficulties at home, Marion moved her to St. Joseph's Manor in Trumbull, Connecticut. Marion thanked Eleanor for her help, although it isn't clear if she helped have her admitted to St. Joseph's, paid some of the costs, or both. In April 1962, some months before Nan's death and her own, Eleanor visited Nan at St. Joseph's and they were photographed with one of the Carmelite sisters (see page 102).

In April 1961 Marion and Nan were deeply concerned to read in the paper that Eleanor was ill, apparently their first knowledge of her serious health issues, though Eleanor's letters were filled with concerns about Nan's declining health. By May, however, Eleanor was clearly unwell, battling acute aplastic anemia, a complication from the spread of infection from an earlier incident of tuberculosis, which for a long time had been inactive.[10] She kept up her schedule the best she could, depending more and more on Edna and David Gurewitsch at home but also unable to persuade David, her doctor, to stop looking for ways to keep her going. In the midst of her own obvious decline, Eleanor arranged for Tubby Curnan to drive her to help Marion with Nan, who was in and out of the hospital. In April and June 1962 Eleanor visited Nan in the nursing home. Nan died at St. Joseph's on 16 August. Eleanor wrote at once to express her condolences, urging Marion to remember that Nan would not have wanted to go on suffering. In October Eleanor wrote to thank Marion for her birthday call and bed jacket, confessing, "I have been miserable since July." It was their last exchange of letters. On 7 November, Eleanor died at her home in New York City.

•

Perhaps those who have loved deeply never stop loving one another. Like the garden, which changes with every season, there is a natural rhythm to human lives and a rootedness buried deep in memory. This story is in homage to Eleanor, Marion, and Nan, and to friends everywhere who may take courage from their lives and find comfort and inspiration in their story.

EPILOGUE

The greatest thing I have learned is how good it is to come home again.
— Eleanor Roosevelt

After months of visibly declining health, Eleanor Roosevelt defied all odds and struggled to keep going. In the summer of 1962, three months before her death, along with her personal secretary Maureen Corr, who for most of a decade had taken Tommy Thompson's place, and David and Edna Gurewitsch, she pushed herself to make one last trip to Campobello for the dedication of the Roosevelt Memorial Bridge, linking Lubec, Maine, to Canada. The Hammer family, which had purchased the Roosevelt cottage from Elliott, invited her to use it, and she flew with family members and friends. When the time came for the dedication, however, Eleanor was too weak to leave the house for the ceremony, and she was represented by her son James.

On the way home by car with Trude Pratt Lash, who had married her friend Joe, a trip she had driven so often herself, she insisted on stopping at her favorite stalls and shops to buy nuts and preserves that she always stocked for Christmas presents. In Castine she stopped at Moss Acre to see Molly Dewson and Polly Porter, and she stopped in Connecticut to see Esther Lape at Salt Meadow. After her visit with Esther, she went on to Val-Kill, where she spent several days, before leaving it forever, returning to New York City. Everyone who saw her recognized that the end was approaching. In and out of the hospital, she was treated by her doctor, David Gurewitsch, and Anna's husband, Dr. James Halsted, whom Anna had married in 1952, but what was left unsaid was obvious to her family: she was dying and there was nothing more they could do (although David never lost hope). Her determination to leave the hospital and to be brought home to her house on East 74th Street was honored, and she arranged for a birthday party for the children. The end came slowly and painfully, as her doctors and family had to come to terms with her stated wish to be allowed to die.

Eleanor Roosevelt died 7 November 1962. She was seventy-eight years old. Marion had taken the train into New York City hoping to see her, and she did visit with her daughter Anna, who was in her mother's home, waiting in the last hours with family and friends for the inevitable end. Marion was unable to see Eleanor. She learned of her death only when she got off the train returning home to New Canaan, just as the news was heard by the public.[1]

Eleanor had made a conscious decision to die in the home she had shared with Edna and David in New York City because she thought it would be hard for family and friends to come to Hyde Park. Her casket was taken to her house at Val-Kill, where family and friends gathered until it was time for the funeral at St. James Episcopal Church in Hyde Park on 10 November 1962. Apparently, Marion did not return to Hyde Park for the service, or at least Eleanor's family does not remember having seen her. Among the many mourners attempting to comfort one another were her granddaughter Ellie and her friend Hick; Hick chose not to be present for the burial but to return to the site after the crowd had dispersed.

Eleanor Roosevelt was buried beside her husband in the rose garden at Springwood. The many guests included President and Mrs. John F. Kennedy, Vice President Lyndon Johnson, former president Harry and Mrs. Truman and their daughter Margaret Truman Daniel, and former president Dwight Eisenhower. Her good friend Adlai Stevenson, whom she had supported in his two campaigns for president, concluded his eulogy in a memorial service at the Cathedral of St. John the Divine in New York City: "Someone has gone from one's own life—who was like the certainty of refuge; and someone has gone from the world—who was like the certainty of honor."[2]

When Nan died on 16 August 1962, a little over a week shy of what would have been her seventy-eighth birthday, a memorial service was held at the Cook family home where Nan grew up and where Eleanor Roosevelt visited at 25 Elm Circle in Massena, New York. She is buried in Pine Grove Cemetery, Massena, in St. Lawrence County, New York.

In news clippings at the Massena History Museum she is remembered as a "Massena girl, closely associated with Mr. and Mrs. Roosevelt." She left a historic record of still photographs and 16-millimeter films of people and places associated with the Roosevelts. They are maintained in the Dickerman-Cook Collection at the Roosevelt-Vanderbilt National Historic Sites and constitute a rare informal look at guests that included FDR and political advisers, family, friends, school children, neighbors, and visiting dignitaries, many of them at Val-Kill picnics.

Marion Dickerman died in Kennett Square, Chester County, Pennsylvania, on 16 May 1983. She was ninety-four years old. She is buried in Westfield Cemetery, Westfield, Chautauqua County, New York. After Marion and Nan had moved to Connecticut, Marion had made a new professional life for herself as education curator at Mystic Seaport. She was invited often to speak publicly about her friendship with the Roosevelts, especially the president. It is a little known fact, however, that Marion was responsible for one of the great tributes to Eleanor Roosevelt. When Eric Gugler was commissioned to create a memorial to Mrs. Roosevelt at the United Nations, he turned for advice to Marion, whom he had known when he was working on architectural changes that Franklin wanted made to the West Wing of the White House. Marion and Gugler had seen one another during Gugler's visits to Hyde Park and Val-Kill.

When Gugler showed Marion a model of what he had in mind, she hesitated to tell him what she thought, until she confessed that she believed he was striving for too much complexity: something simple seemed to her to be the appropriate way to honor Eleanor Roosevelt. She told him about the times that she and Eleanor had gone to Rock Creek Cemetery in Washington, D.C., where Eleanor found such comfort in the simplicity and dignity of a particular memorial.[3] It was Eleanor's favorite place in Washington, and she took special friends with her to sit in silence on the half-circular stone bench, there to gaze upon the Adams Memorial, a large bronze statue designed for Henry Adams by Augustus Saint-Gaudens in memory of Henry's wife, Clover. In the serenity of a grove of evergreens and in the strength of a woman's face, Eleanor had learned self-mastery for her own life's journey.[4]

Following Marion's suggestion, Gugler returned to his task, and when it was done he wrote to thank her for her help. On 23 April 1966, the monument was dedicated by the Eleanor Roosevelt Memorial Foundation on the northeast corner of the United Nations Garden. It consists of a wide semicircular granite bench and faces a tall slab with a bas-relief of a flame bearing Adlai Stevenson's words, "She would rather light a candle than curse the darkness and her glow has warmed the world."

•

Today, visitors to the National Park Service's Eleanor Roosevelt National Historic Site at Val-Kill in Hyde Park can tour the modest place Eleanor called home. It is a stucco building—awkward in its various additions—that was once the furniture factory, in close proximity to the stone cottage she shared with Marion and Nan. As soon as one steps inside, there is great charm and warmth. It feels as if Mrs. Roosevelt is at home.

Here we can imagine the life she lived, reflected in the simplicity and beauty of the knotty pine walls, the many photographs and prints, the books, furniture (much of it made in the shop), the porches, and the crooked lampshades, as if someone had just closed a book and turned off the light. Here is where Mrs. Roosevelt and John F. Kennedy had tea when he came to ask for her support in his presidential bid; here Ethiopian emperor Haile Selassie sat with his shoes off, resting as he watched a small television screen; here she and Tommy Thompson worked tirelessly on her books and correspondence. Comfortable sofas and chairs are for sitting by the fire. The dining table is set for guests. Up a narrow flight of stairs are a narrow hall and a nest of small rooms for Eleanor's many guests. Her own bedroom is connected to a sleeping porch that faces the pond, where she liked to sleep in all kinds of weather. It looks down upon Stone Cottage. The bedroom is filled with photographs of family and friends, over the mantel and bed.

With her death in 1962, the children sold off the Roosevelt properties and put much of the contents of the houses for sale at auction. New owners turned the shop into rental units and began to develop the property without restriction as to use. Elliott had sold property across Albany Post Road for a drive-in theater.

In 1975 an impassioned group of concerned citizens stopped further desecration by raising the alarm and the funds to preserve the historic site. President Jimmy Carter signed the bill that created the Eleanor Roosevelt Historic Site. Ever since, National Park Service rangers have guided thousands of visitors through her home, filled again with what she loved.

Next door, Stone Cottage, as it is identified by the National Park Service that maintains it, exhibits Eleanor's desk, Nan's woodworking tools, and silver monogrammed with E M N. On a flickering screen Nan's home movies show Marion tousling Nan's hair and other happy times with the Roosevelts and many guests. Even in the empty spaces, there are echoes of a life lived.

•

After the last visitor has gone, as we stand on the bridge, listen to the creek and the birds, and breathe in the air, we can live momentarily in the world where Eleanor, Marion, and Nan lived: it seems timeless— unchanged and enduring. Later, the moon will rise, and the cottage will seem to float upon water.

ACKNOWLEDGMENTS

I first sought to learn the art of writing biography on the recommendation of Walter Beeker, that volcanic source of information for all his friends, who recommended that I read *Yankee from Olympus: Justice Holmes and His Family*, by Catherine Drinker Bowen, published in 1945. I often reread it to freshen my nib, to borrow Virginia Woolf's graphic phrase.

Over many years I have read books about Eleanor and Franklin Roosevelt; visited on several occasions the historic sites at Hyde Park, New York, and the Roosevelt Campobello International Park in New Brunswick, Canada; worked in the archives at the Franklin D. Roosevelt Presidential Library and Museum at Hyde Park (FDRL) and the National Park Service (NPS) archives of the Roosevelt-Vanderbilt National Historic Sites; and studied hundreds of historical documents.

The transcripts of two long interviews in particular were of special importance, both at the Columbia Center for Oral History, Rare Book and Manuscript Library, Columbia University, New York City: one with Marion Dickerman and the other with Frances Perkins. A unique document is Esther Lape's unpublished memoir "Salt Meadow: From the Perspective of a Half Century" (Lape Papers, FDRL).

Readers interested in learning more about Eleanor Roosevelt will find an abundance of published sources. I recommend starting with the first two autobiographies by Eleanor Roosevelt: *This Is My Story* and *This I Remember*. The most recent reissue of these two volumes in one book is *The Autobiography of Eleanor Roosevelt*. Eleanor's small book of her father's letters, *Hunting Big Game in the Eighties*, is an especially revealing and endearing portrait of daughter and father as she wanted him to be remembered. Readers will enjoy her "My Day" columns (1936–62), easily available in the electronic edition of the Eleanor Roosevelt Papers Project, George Washington University, Washington, D.C. The project director and editor, Christopher Black, is a most generous and dependable resource. My favorite book about one of Eleanor's children is *Mother and Daughter: The Letters of Eleanor and Anna Roosevelt*, edited by Bernard Asbell; a companion volume is *A Love in Shadow: The Story of Anna Roosevelt and John Boettiger*, told by their son John R. Boettiger. An extremely useful book to keep on hand is *The Eleanor Roosevelt Encyclopedia*, edited by Maurine H. Beasley, Holly C. Shulman, and Henry R. Beasley.

Among the books that have most informed my own understanding are those by Eleanor's great friend Joseph Lash, who met her when he was in his thirties and remained a close friend until her death. Lash's books include *Eleanor Roosevelt: A Friend's Memoir*; *Eleanor and Franklin: The Story of Their Relationship, Based on Eleanor Roosevelt's Private Papers*; *Love, Eleanor: Eleanor Roosevelt and Her Friends*; *A World of Love: Eleanor Roosevelt and Her Friends, 1943–1962*; and *Eleanor, the Years Alone*.

Absolutely essential to our understanding of Eleanor Roosevelt is the monumental three-volume biography of Eleanor Roosevelt by Blanche Wiesen Cook. We are all in Cook's debt for her years of research and travel, as well as for her readable prose style, and her wise understanding of Eleanor, her friends and family, and American history. For readers who can't travel to Hyde Park to read documents in the FDRL archives (with new ones being digitized every year), Cook has provided an invaluable service in quoting from so many letters in these three volumes.

I admire especially the research and writing of Geoffrey C. Ward, recommended to me by my son, and I have read closely his two biographies of the early years: *Before the Trumpet: Young Franklin Roosevelt, 1882–1905* and *A First-Class Temperament: The Emergence of Franklin Roosevelt, 1905–1928*. A remarkable book, *Closest Companion: The Unknown Story of the Intimate Friendship of Franklin Roosevelt and Margaret Suckley*, edited by Ward, gives a personal perspective of FDR I have not found in other books. I enjoyed with millions of other viewers Ward's collaboration with Ken Burns on the PBS documentary *The Roosevelts*, as well as the published text. I also found helpful *The Woman behind the New Deal: The Life of Frances Perkins, FDR's Secretary of Labor and His Moral Conscience*, by

Kirstin Downey, and Perkins's own memoir, *The Roosevelt I Knew*. Another favorite book of mine is *A Volume of Friendship: The Letters of Eleanor Roosevelt and Isabella Greenway, 1904–1953*, edited by Kristie Miller and Robert H. McGinnis. Doris Kearns Goodwin is a spellbinding writer, and she has brought her genius for storytelling to *No Ordinary Time: Franklin and Eleanor Roosevelt: The Home Front in World War II*.

There are many good essays about Eleanor Roosevelt. I recommend especially "Biographical Sketch" by William H. Chafe and "ER and Democratic Politics: Women in the Postsuffrage Era" by Susan Ware, published in *Without Precedent: The Life and Career of Eleanor Roosevelt*, edited by Joan Hoff-Wilson and Marjorie Lightman; also Allida Black's comprehensive introduction in the 2012 Penguin reprint of *Tomorrow Is Now*.

Susan Ware has brought her focus as a feminist historian to bear upon the life of Eleanor Roosevelt in a timely and visionary way. Ware's book that has meant the most to my understanding of the way single women lived is *Partner and I: Molly Dewson, Feminism, and New Deal Politics*. I am especially indebted to Ware for helping me make contact with Dewson's great-niece, Virginia Bourne, and her husband, Standish, so that my husband, daughter Sally, and I could visit the family home in Castine, Maine, where Eleanor, Marion, and Nan had been guests.

Among other biographers I admire is Kenneth S. Davis, who combines a unique literary style with meticulous research. The book I found most useful of his is *FDR: The New York Years, 1928–1933*. Davis is also the historian who first made use of oral history interviews that Mary Bell Starr conducted with Marion Dickerman for the Columbia Center for Oral History, which were the main primary sources for the writing of this book. Parts of those long interviews together with his own interviews with Marion Dickerman became the basis for Davis's book *Invincible Summer: An Intimate Portrait of the Roosevelts Based on the Recollections of Marion Dickerman*, which includes many of Nancy Cook's photographs and movie stills. It rightly is dedicated to Nancy Cook. I have gone back and forth between those two sources as a way of recognizing the work of both Starr and Davis, who so many years ago thought to interview Marion Dickerman, the last surviving member of the "Three Graces."

Nan's family members Gary and Bonnie Cook in Massena, New York, gave me access to photographs and clippings I otherwise would have missed. Several Roosevelt family members and friends have been especially kind. Edna Gurewitsch talked with me on the phone several times about the friendship that she and her husband, Dr. David Gurewitsch, shared with Eleanor Roosevelt and gave me the best advice: to trust my own instincts. Her book *Kindred Souls: The Devoted Friendship of Eleanor Roosevelt and Dr. David Gurewitsch* shows us how Eleanor lived in the last years of her life in the New York brownstone she shared with the Gurewitsches. Eleanor's granddaughters Ellie Roosevelt Seagraves and Nina Roosevelt Gibson were generously forthcoming in sharing their memories of their beloved grandmother, always interested even when I was asking questions they have answered over many years. Talking on the phone and e-mailing with them were some of the highlights of my research. One of the first people I met in the Roosevelt circle was Malvina "Tommy" Thompson's niece and Eleanor's goddaughter, Eleanor "Ellie" Zartman, whom I visited in her home in Maryland, introduced by her friend, the poet Judith Bowles.

Finally, any scholar or reader wanting to know more about the Roosevelts should go to the excellent website of the Franklin D. Roosevelt Presidential Library and Museum at Hyde Park, which offers a virtual tour of exhibits and has thousands of documents and photographs already digitized and free and open to the public. Many staff members have been unfailingly helpful in answering numerous questions, making copies of requested documents, and pointing me in the right directions. An especially memorable evening at Hyde Park was the night my family and I heard Geoffrey Ward speak at the Wallace Visitor and Education Center. The motor trips to Hyde Park for me and my husband were made possible by our able drivers and boon companions, our daughters, Sally and Julie.

My favorite Roosevelt resource is the Val-Kill site itself, both Stone

Cottage and the house (the renovated furniture shop) that is the Eleanor Roosevelt National Historic Site. In addition, the site's website provides a fine virtual tour of the house itself. There is an excellent exhibit in Stone Cottage and a guided tour of the house Eleanor called home until her death in 1962.

I want to hold up for praise and thanks a number of NPS professionals at the Roosevelt-Vanderbilt National Historic Sites. Sarah Olson, superintendent of the site, welcomed me to the U.S. Park Service office in the Bellefield house. At Bellefield Anne Jordan, the chief curator, also made room in her busy schedule to talk with me about Eleanor Roosevelt. I will always remember her generous insights and encouragement. I thank especially Michele Ballos and Tara McGill, who allowed me to work at my best times in the NPS archive and generously copied documents. The Marion Dickerman Papers belong to the NPS archive, many of which were copied from the originals for the FDRL archives. In particular, NPS staff members Franceska Macsali Urbin and Frank Futral have been my most knowledgeable and generous compatriots in this journey to Val-Kill, and without them I would have been a lonely visitor. Franceska was a careful and generous reader from the beginning. Michele Ballos and Tara McGill welcomed me to work in the Marion Dickerman collection at the Roosevelt-Vanderbilt National Historic Sites, continued to send me many documents and images in the mail, and were always kind to answer more questions. I also had lovely walks at Val-Kill with Anna deCordova, NPS horticulturist, who is working to restore a sense of active use to Val-Kill circa 1950s. When I visited, the cutting garden restoration was complete and the staff was planning the swimming pool and tennis court restoration. Kathleen Durham, executive director of the Eleanor Roosevelt Center at Val-Kill, was especially welcoming in her office near the historic site.

Many archivists in libraries, churches, and municipal offices have responded to my requests for information. I thank especially those at the Massena Museum in Massena, New York; Vassar College; Wellesley College; Smith College; Syracuse University; and Patterson

Library, Westfield, New York. Jeanne Goodman and Jeri Diehl Cusack have provided information about the New Deal resettlement project at Arthurdale, West Virginia. My favorite library is always the Z. Smith Reynolds Library of Wake Forest University.

Encouragers have been Richard Cain, whose great-grandparents, Moses and Hattie Smith, rented land from FDR and who grew up at Val-Kill. Cain is the primary collector of Val-Kill furniture and pewter, has written a book about Val-Kill (*Eleanor Roosevelt's Val-Kill*), and was always willing to help answer questions.

My friends are a wellspring of help and inspiration, as her friends were to Eleanor Roosevelt. I am always grateful to David Link, who refreshes my garden and my wood pile and brings me honey from his hives, which make a long workday especially pleasant. Special thanks to my friend Irv Gellman, who helped me write a better proposal after we met at a biography conference; Paula Duggan, Penelope Niven, Deanne Urmy, Barbara Hogenson, Robert Morgan, the members of my writers' group, Bio Brio—Margaret Supplee Smith, Michele Gillespie, and Anna Rubino; Sue Quinn, Laura Fennell, Katherine Gill, Florence Gatten, Susan Whittington, Lawrence Womack, Jill Game Carraway, and Deborah Horning; Nick Bragg; members of the Ada Leake Myers Book Club and the Gang of Four; members of St. Anne's Episcopal Church; members of the Democratic Party; Sudie Duncan Sides; Betty Nash McIver Luning, Heather Ross Miller, and Isabel Zuber; Howard Shields and Anne Kesler Shields; Louise Gossett; Ruth and Tom Mullen, Jean Burroughs, Martha Fleer, and Norma-Mae Isakow; Susan Faust and Betsy Gregg; Elen Knott, Marsha McGregor, Joanne Wyckoff, Rebecca McClanahan, Kenneth Frazelle, Rick Mashburn, Clifton and Anna Mathews, Kathryn Milam, and Jane Hatcher; my doctor, Heidi Klepin; and Korea Allah, my spiritual adviser. I learned from Eleanor Roosevelt how important it is to make new (younger) friends. I hold up for special thanks writer Helen Humphreys, whose research on my great-great-great-great-great grandmother, miraculously, brought her from Canada to North Carolina, connecting my interest in women's history over two centuries.

It has been an honor to work with staff members of the University of North Carolina Press. I have had no finer editor than Mark Simpson-Vos, the kindest as well as the most astute. Jessica Newman and Mary Carley Caviness and freelance editor Trish Watson were exceptional in helping me ready the manuscript for publication. On the production and design side, Kim Bryant and Rich Hendel have been masters of the art.

I am especially grateful to Jackson Smith for help preparing the photographs.

My life is centered in my North Carolina home and family. They entertain, educate, and sustain me: Ed, my husband of fifty-three years and best reader, to whom this book is dedicated; Ed Wilson Jr. (Eddie) and Laurie Turnage Wilson, and their four children—Ed III (Buddy), Harry, Maria, and Eleanor (Ellie); Sally Wilson and Carolyn Stevenson; and Julie Wilson and John Steele. In them I know the meaning of love.

I could not have written this book without Mindy Conner, my genius book editor. Mindy, we did it, and are still friends (and neighbors). In editing and formatting the manuscript, you did what you promised—you carried me across the finish line.

Finally, I wrote this book in homage to Eleanor Roosevelt, Marion Dickerman, and Nancy Cook, and to women everywhere whose friendships for one another have been a sustaining force in their lives.

Winston-Salem, N.C.

Summer 2016

TIMELINE

1884	Nancy Cook is born 26 August in Massena, New York.
1884	Eleanor Roosevelt is born 11 October in New York City.
1890	Marion Dickerman is born 11 April in Westfield, New York.
1892	Eleanor's mother, Anna Hall Roosevelt, dies.
1894	Eleanor's father, Elliott Roosevelt, dies.
1899–1902	Eleanor attends Allenswood in England.
1905	Eleanor marries Franklin D. Roosevelt 17 March in New York City.
1906	Daughter Anna is born 3 May.
1907	Son James is born 23 December.
1909	Son Franklin Jr. is born 18 March; dies 8 November.
1910	Son Elliott is born 23 September.
1912	Nancy Cook and Marion Dickerman graduate from Syracuse University.
1913–18	Nancy Cook and Marion Dickerman teach at Fulton High School in Fulton, New York.
1913	Eleanor, FDR, and family move to Washington, D.C., where FDR serves in the Wilson administration as assistant secretary of the navy.
1914	Son Franklin Jr. is born 17 August on Campobello Island.
1916	Son John is born 17 March.
1917–18	Eleanor volunteers with American Red Cross canteens in Washington, D.C., during World War I.
1918–19	Nancy Cook and Marion Dickerman work at Endell Street Military Hospital in London.
1918	Eleanor discovers Lucy Mercer's letters to Franklin.
1919	Marion Dickerman runs for New York State Assembly, losing but making a strong showing in a campaign managed by Nancy Cook.
1920	Congress passes the Nineteenth Amendment granting women the right to vote.
1921	Franklin is stricken with polio on Campobello Island.

1922	Eleanor joins the Women's Trade Union League and the Women's Division of the New York State Democratic Committee; she meets Marion Dickerman and Nancy Cook.
1922	Marion Dickerman joins faculty at Todhunter School in New York City; Nancy Cook serves as executive secretary of the Women's Division of the New York State Democratic Committee.
1923	Eleanor works with Esther Lape to organize the Bok Peace Prize competition and studies League of Women Voters issues with Lape's partner, Elizabeth Read.
1924	Eleanor plays leading role in Al Smith's third bid for New York governor.
1925	Eleanor edits *Women's Democratic News* with Caroline O'Day, Marion Dickerman, Nancy Cook, and Elinor Morgenthau. The women travel together organizing Democratic women in New York State.
1925–26	Eleanor, Marion, and Nan build cottage on the Val-Kill at Hyde Park, celebrating completion 1 January 1926. They begin summer travels to Campobello Island with Roosevelt children.
1926	Franklin purchases property at Warm Springs, Georgia.
1926	Val-Kill furniture factory opens under Nan's direction.
1927	Eleanor, Marion, and Nan (as a silent partner) purchase Todhunter School in New York City. Eleanor begins teaching, later commuting from the governor's mansion in Albany two and a half days a week.
1928–32	FDR is governor of New York.
1929	Eleanor, Marion, and Nan take youngest Roosevelt boys on a long European tour.
1932	FDR is elected president of the United States in November. Eleanor begins friendship with Lorena Hickok. Marion and Nan become part of the inner circle of White House family guests.
1932	Eleanor rents an apartment at 20th East 11th Street in Greenwich Village, a brownstone owned by Esther Lape and Elizabeth Read.
1933	Eleanor resigns from the faculty at Todhunter School as she becomes First Lady.
1933	FDR is inaugurated 4 March. On 6 March Eleanor hosts first weekly press conference for women reporters. Eleanor and Nan

        begin traveling to Arthurdale near Morgantown, West Virginia,
        to support resettlement housing project at Scotts Run.

1935   Eleanor begins "My Day" newspaper column 30 December.

1936   FDR is elected to a second term. Eleanor begins a paid lecture
        tour. Val-Kill furniture factory closes. Eleanor renovates the shop
        into a home for herself and her secretary, Malvina Thompson.
        Louis Howe, FDR's friend and closest political adviser, dies.

1937   Eleanor publishes first volume of her autobiography,
        This Is My Story

1938   Eleanor withdraws her name from the Todhunter School.
        Eleanor, Marion, and Nan negotiate property settlements.

1939   Todhunter merges with the Dalton School, and Marion becomes
        associate principal.

1940   FDR is elected to a third term. Nan and Marion continue to help
        Eleanor host presidential picnics at Val-Kill.

1941   FDR Library at Hyde Park is dedicated. Nan resigns as executive
        secretary of the Women's Division of the New York Democratic
        party. On 7 September Sara Delano Roosevelt dies; on 25
        September Eleanor's brother Hall Roosevelt dies.

1942   Marion leaves Todhunter (now merged with the Dalton School)
        and takes temporary teaching jobs.

1944   Marguerite "Missy" LeHand, private secretary to FDR, dies after
        having been several years incapacitated by illness.

1945   FDR is elected to a fourth term; he dies 12 April at Warm Springs.
        Eleanor is appointed U.S. delegate to the United Nations by
        President Harry S. Truman. On 21 November the family gives
        Springwood to the U.S. government to be maintained by the
        National Park Service.

1946–52 Elliott Roosevelt and his wife, Faye Emerson, move into Top
        Cottage, which FDR and Daisy Suckley had designed as their
        retirement home; Elliott goes into a farming operation with his
        mother. Elliott sells Top Cottage and other Roosevelt properties
        and leaves Hyde Park.

1947–51 Eleanor chairs the Commission on Human Rights of the
        United Nations.

1947	Marion and Nan move to New Canaan, Connecticut, on 2 October.
1948	Eleanor presents Universal Declaration of Human Rights for adoption by the General Assembly of the United Nations.
1949	Elinor Morgenthau dies 21 September.
1952	John Roosevelt and his family move to Stone Cottage.
1953	Malvina Thompson dies 12 April.
1962	Nancy Cook dies in Trumbull, Connecticut, on 16 August. Eleanor dies in New York City on 7 November.
1970	John Roosevelt sells Stone Cottage. Elliott Roosevelt sells Top Cottage and other Roosevelt properties.
1973	Local citizens lead effort to save Eleanor's home at Val-Kill from commercial development.
1977	Federal legislation creates the Eleanor Roosevelt National History Site at Val-Kill.
1981	Esther Lape dies 17 May.
1983	Marion Dickerman dies in Kennett Square, Pennsylvania, 16 May.
1984	Eleanor Roosevelt National Historic Site dedicated.
2014	Stone Cottage exhibit "Eleanor Roosevelt and Val-Kill: Emergence of a Political Leader" opens.

NOTES

Abbreviations

AERP   Anna Eleanor Roosevelt Papers, Franklin D. Roosevelt
Presidential Library and Museum, Hyde Park, N.Y.,

CCOH   Columbia Center for Oral History, Butler Library, New York, N.Y.

ER   Eleanor Roosevelt

EROHP   Eleanor Roosevelt Oral History Project, Franklin D. Roosevelt
Presidential Library and Museum, Hyde Park, N.Y.

ERPP   Eleanor Roosevelt Papers Project, George Washington University,
Washington, D.C., https://www2.gwu.edu/~erpapers/documents/

FDR   Franklin Delano Roosevelt

FDRL   Franklin D. Roosevelt Presidential Library and Museum, Hyde
Park, N.Y.

MD   Marion Dickerman

MDP   Marion Dickerman Papers, Franklin D. Roosevelt Presidential
Library and Museum, Hyde Park, N.Y.

NC   Nancy Cook

Prologue

1. Quoted in Morris, *Miss Wylie of Vassar*, 154.

2. ER, *Autobiography*, 427. I have found the 2014 Harper Perennial reprint of this book to be the most useful for today's readers, available in paperback and on Kindle.

Chapter One

1. Quoted in Ward, *Before the Trumpet*, 153–54. The descriptions of Hyde Park are based on factual evidence and visits to the places described. The history of James and Sara Delano Roosevelt is told in many sources. I found especially useful Ward, *Before the Trumpet*; Davis, *FDR: The Beckoning of Destiny*; and Steeholm and Steeholm, *House at Hyde Park*. Fredriksen, *Our Local Heritage*, is also useful, as is a short history of St. James Episcopal Church given me by the Reverend Chuck Kramer and an interview with the Reverend Gordon Kidd, in EROHP. Suckley, "Day at Hyde Park," has a unique perspective and

is not often cited. Moody, *FDR and His Hudson Valley Neighbors*, includes a good deal of information.

2. ER, "My Day," 24 August 1936. All of ER's "My Day" columns are available at ERPP.

3. In using the word "crippled," which some today regard as offensive, I am following the lead of James Tobin (*Man He Became*, 9), who chose "after a good deal of thought" to describe FDR's disability in the language used at the time.

Chapter Two

1. Blanche Wiesen Cook begins her three-volume biography of ER by quoting what those who met ER described as her effect upon an audience — "her very presence lit up the room" (*Eleanor Roosevelt*, 1:1–2). I have heard her effect upon an audience similarly described by my fellow alumnae at the Woman's College of the University of North Carolina (present-day UNC-Greensboro), where ER often visited her friend Dean Harriet Elliott. The 1922 meeting of ER and NC at a political fund-raiser for the Women's Division of the New York State Democratic Committee is briefly described in several sources. A place to begin is Cook, *Eleanor Roosevelt*, 1:319–20. I have researched the lives of MD and NC in many available sources, including my correspondence with NC's family; the Massena Museum in Massena, New York; the Patterson Library of Westfield, New York; and ERPP. Published sources of particular use are Davis, *Invincible Summer*; and Lash, *Eleanor and Franklin*.

2. Quoted in Lash, *Eleanor and Franklin*, 278.

3. ER to Isabella Greenway, 26 October 1919, in Miller and McGinnis, *Volume of Friendship*, 170.

4. Isabella Greenway to ER, 29 December 1921, in ibid., 185.

5. The story of the romance of FDR and Lucy Mercer (Rutherfurd) is told in many places. One of the most recent retellings is Rowley, *Franklin and Eleanor*.

6. Cook, *Eleanor Roosevelt*, 1:292–93.

7. Lash, *Eleanor and Franklin*, 278.

8. Quoted in Roosevelt, *Grandmère*, 37.

9. ER to FDR, 29 June 1922, FDRL. Blanche Wiesen Cook and other Roosevelt scholars often cite FDRL letters only by name and date, a style I have followed here. The Roosevelt archives at FDRL contain finding aids that will enable readers to search the collections further; my research has been made

challenging because there is no single source or concentrated batch of detailed information pertaining to the time period that is the focus of this book. Materials are scattered across the vast holdings, and often one document appears in different collections. Staff members are especially helpful in this process. Most of the letters used in this book are from the papers of ER, FDR, and MD, and my citations to those collections should be the most useful to readers.

10. Quoted in Lash, *Eleanor and Franklin*, 261.

11. MD oral history, CCOH. I have not included page numbers to the MD oral history at CCOH because they are either missing from the transcripts or altered and therefore are very difficult to follow. Much of the same material appears in interviews by Kenneth S. Davis published in *Invincible Summer*, for which I do give page numbers.

12. Davis, *Invincible Summer*, 17.

13. "Massena Girl Associated with Mrs. Roosevelt in Unique Shop," n.d., vertical file, Massena History Museum, Massena, N.Y.

14. Davis, *Invincible Summer*, 4.

15. ER, *Autobiography*, 123.

16. Ibid., 143.

17. Quoted in Davis, *Invincible Summer*, 31.

18. Frances Perkins oral history, CCOH. The CCOH website (http://library.columbia.edu/locations/ccoh.html) has an excellent search engine directing readers to specific pages of this long digital transcription.

19. Anna Roosevelt Cowles to Corinne Roosevelt Robinson, 11 December 1923, Anna Roosevelt Cowles Papers, letters, folder 7, Houghton Library, Harvard University, Cambridge, Mass.

Chapter Three

1. MD oral history, CCOH. The name "Val-Kill" comes from the Fall-Kill Creek. We understand that the Dutch pronounced Fall-Kill "Val-Kill." The name "Stone Cottage" was never used at the time ER, MD, and NC built it, though it was sometimes referred to as "the stone cottage." The National Park Service now uses that name to distinguish the two main buildings—the stone cottage and the renovated shop next door that is now the Eleanor Roosevelt National Historic Site. When ER converted the factory into her home and used the stone cottage for her children and grandchildren, she called

them the Val-Kill Cottages. After FDR died and MD and NC left, ER considered the whole place Val-Kill and the whole place her home. This chapter is based largely on the long interviews with MD, both at CCOH and in Davis's *Invincible Summer*. I have also consulted Davis's notes for the interviews in the Kenneth S. Davis Papers at Kansas State University.

2. Quoted in Davis, *Invincible Summer*, 35.

Chapter Four

1. Sara Delano Roosevelt's journey to Campobello is described in Ward, *First-Class Temperament*, 593. Sources on Campobello include Nowlan, *Campobello*; and Klein, *Beloved Island*. Elen Knott's books and her descriptions of her summer home at Lubec, Maine, and my visit with my family to Campobello informed much of my appreciation for this region.

2. Lash, *Love, Eleanor*, 67–68.

3. Nina Roosevelt Gibson, e-mail to the author, 16 January 2015.

4. Eleanor Roosevelt Seagraves, e-mail to the author, 12 November 2015.

5. Quoted in Gurewitsch, *Kindred Souls*, 48.

6. Journal entry date 18 July 1925, quoted in Lash, *Love, Eleanor*, 93.

Chapter Five

1. Pearson, *Historic Structure Report*. Important, neglected information in this chapter shows how much FDR was involved in the construction of the cottage: receipts are in the FDR Papers Pertaining to Family, Business, and Personal Affairs, 1882, 1945, series 4: Financial Papers, 1903–43, box 60, FDRL. In addition to the principal source for this chapter—the interviews with MD—I have studied several publications from the National Park Service. Among them are Pearson, *Historic Structure Report*; Lisa Nowak, *Cultural Landscape Report for Eleanor Roosevelt National Historic Site*, vol. 1 (2005); and Emily Wright and Katherine B. Menz, *Historic Furnishings Report/Eleanor Roosevelt/Val-Kill* (1986).

2. The letter is in the FDR Papers Pertaining to Family, Business, and Personal Affairs. All other information about the costs of the construction is from this file.

3. Ward, *First-Class Temperament*, 736–37.

4. MD oral history, CCOH.

5. ER to FDR, 12 April 1926, FDRL.

6. In 1952 the Hammer family purchased the Roosevelt property at Campobello Island and later donated it to the United States and Canada. Hammer's company also handled Roosevelt estate sales. MD oral history, CCOH.

7. Several engagement books, diaries, and address and dinner books, which yield little information on activities in the early years at Val-Kill, are housed within AERP, most still in their original bindings. ER's primary schedule materials are currently contained in boxes 4 and 10, AERP. I am grateful to Kirsten Carter, digital archivist at FDRL, for describing these materials to me.

8. I am indebted to Eleanor Roosevelt Seagraves for this insight.

9. ER to MD, 18 May 1926 and 27 August 1925, MDP.

10. Sara Delano Roosevelt to FDR, 2 April 1926, FDRL.

11. Miller and McGinnis, *Volume of Friendship*, 160.

12. ER to MD, 18 May 1926, MDP.

13. ER to MD, 14 August 1925, MDP.

14. Quoted in Lash, *Eleanor and Franklin*, 342.

15. Ward, *First-Class Temperament*, 755.

Chapter Six

1. ER to FDR, 26 April 1926, FDRL. Pearson, *Historic Structure Report*, was especially useful in writing this chapter. For my understanding of so many aspects of Stone Cottage and Val-Kill I am especially grateful to Franceska Mascali Urbin, supervisory park ranger at the Home of Franklin D. Roosevelt and Eleanor Roosevelt National Historic Sites; and Frank Futral, curator, Roosevelt-Vanderbilt National Historic Sites.

2. MD oral history, CCOH.

3. Ibid.

4. Ibid.

5. Ward, *First-Class Temperament*, 740.

6. From ER's personal letter to Joseph P. Lash, 25 October 1941 in Lash, *Eleanor and Franklin*, 220.

7. There is factual evidence for the details of this scene. For example, a home movie as part of an exhibit at Stone Cottage today shows MD affectionately tousling NC's hair.

8. Quotations are from Davis, *Invincible Summer*, 65.

9. Alice Roosevelt Longworth, cited in Ward, *First-Class Temperament*, 631.

10. Especially important for an understanding of FDR and Margaret "Daisy" Suckley is Ward, *Closest Companion*.

Chapter Seven

1. My evocation of what I imagine might have been ER's visit to the cemetery is based on my own time at St. James Episcopal Church on the Albany Post Road in Hyde Park and my familiarity as an Episcopalian with the Book of Common Prayer. The Reverend Chuck Kramer at St. James has been a knowledgeable and lively e-mail correspondent, sharing his thoughts about ER's religious life. I am grateful for that understanding. An interview with Reverend Gordon Kidd in EROHP also helps describe St. James and Mrs. Roosevelt's church membership.

2. Visitors to Hyde Park usually begin their tours at Springwood, the Roosevelt "Big House," which belonged to FDR and his mother and never felt like home to ER. But for our setting, we must take a two-mile walk or short ride on the eastern part of Hyde Park to Val-Kill, where the landscape is decidedly different, with fields, forests, gardens, stream and pond, Stone Cottage, and the Eleanor Roosevelt National Historic Site, where tours are given. A visit to St. James Episcopal Church and cemetery completes this important journey.

Chapter Eight

1. Quoted in Morris, *Miss Wylie of Vassar*, 134.

2. Martha Gellhorn interview, EROHP, 1.

3. Quoted in Cook, *Eleanor Roosevelt*, 1:222.

4. I am especially indebted to Jan Scholl for her interesting e-mails about the research she is doing on Martha Van Rensselaer.

5. Same-sex relationships within the home economics movement are examined in Megan Elias, "'Model Mamas': The Domestic Partnership of Home Economics Pioneers Flora Rose and Martha Van Rensselaer," *Journal of the History of Sexuality* 15 (January 2006): 65–88 ("a more perfect society," 65).

6. Martha Van Rensselaer to ER, 4 April 1930, AERP.

7. Laura Shapiro, "The First Kitchen," *New Yorker*, 22 November 2010.

8. Carrie Chapman Catt to Martha Van Rensselaer, 21 November 1925, Cornell University Library digital archives, Ithaca, N.Y.

9. Susan Ware observed that ER's pattern was "to move on, imperceptibly,

to new friends and new issues, leaving old friendships intact but without the centrality (at least to the other person) they had held earlier." In this discussion Ware argues that "nothing ever matched the intensity" of ER and Molly's friendship during the 1932 campaign and the early days of the New Deal (*Letter to the World*, 24).

10. Copies of the Dewson-Porter scrapbooks are housed in the Schlesinger Library of the Radcliffe Institute for Advanced Study, Harvard University.

11. Molly Dewson to ER, July 1936, AERP, quoted in Ware, *Partner and I*, 220.

12. Until we know more about the Lape-Read-Roosevelt friendship, we cannot know the whole story. When Lape becomes the subject of a deserving biography, however, its author will have the benefit of newly obtained papers of Esther Lape's donated by two of Lape's friends to Blanche Wiesen Cook for her third and final volume of her biography *Eleanor Roosevelt* (2016). They will go to the FDRL.

13. Quoted in Lash, *Eleanor and Franklin*, 287.

14. Esther Lape, "Salt Meadow: From the Perspective of a Half Century," Lape Papers, 78, FDRL.

15. Lash, *Eleanor and Franklin*, 280.

16. Cook gives the fullest analysis of anti-Semitism and the Roosevelts in *Eleanor Roosevelt*, vol. 2, chap. 16.

17. ER to FDR, 27 April 1928, FDRL.

18. In *Love, Eleanor* (115–23), Joseph Lash described his interviews with Earl Miller when Earl was seventy years old and living alone in Florida, where ER had sometimes been his house guest. Lash's account is the closest we may get to understanding the relationship.

Chapter Nine

1. *It's Up to the Women* was the title of a book ER published in 1933, her first. In 1927 she made a list of seven points in an unpublished article she called "Ethics of Parents," including "have bigness of soul." It appears in Lash, *Eleanor and Franklin*, 193.

2. ER's grandson, Elliott's son David B. Roosevelt, wrote in *Grandmère* about his memories and those of some of his cousins, making use of the FDRL archives. Nancy Roosevelt Ireland has been interviewed for television documentaries on the Roosevelts.

3. MD oral history, CCOH.

4. ER to MD, MDP, quoted in Cook, *Eleanor Roosevelt*, 1:329; Rose Schneiderman, with Lucy Goldthwaite, *All for One*, quoted in Beasley, Shulman, and Beasley, *Eleanor Roosevelt Encyclopedia*, 475.

5. MD oral history, CCOH.

6. Ibid.

7. Nina Roosevelt Gibson, e-mail to the author, 29 July 2015. Also lively and informative is an interview with Nina Roosevelt Gibson in EROHP.

Chapter Ten

1. Beasley, *Eleanor Roosevelt and the Media*, provides the fullest account of ER's efforts as a journalist.

2. Caroline O'Day, *Democratic Women's News*, November 1925, New York Public Library.

3. The most comprehensive study of Val-Kill Industries is Futral, "Val-Kill Industries," 21–39. Richard Cain, who grew up at Val-Kill, was a great help in sharing his memories and his knowledge of the products produced in the shop, including his own large collection.

4. A useful document is the Otto Berge oral history interview, Roosevelt-Vanderbilt National Historic Sites. The staff of the National Park Service generously made copies of this and other interviews about Val-Kill. Berge made clear his lack of respect for NC as manager of the factory and his respect for Mrs. Roosevelt.

5. A short but useful discussion of ER's "taste for entrepreneurship" and the money she made as a freelance writer, lecturer, and radio personality is in Ware, *Letter to the World*, 35–37.

Chapter Eleven

1. Cook, *Eleanor Roosevelt*, 2:316. Boxes of materials in AERP and MDP offer detailed information about Todhunter and ER's assignments. See Cook, *Eleanor Roosevelt*, 1:397–408, for the most comprehensive history of ER at Todhunter.

2. ER to MD, 7 February 1926, MDP.

3. Class notes, AERP, box 7.

4. Anne Ward Gilbert interview, 20 September 1978, EROHP.

Chapter Twelve

1. The digitized "My Day" columns at ERPP are an especially useful source of information on ER's daily activities after 1935.

2. Lorena Hickok's biography, *Eleanor Roosevelt: Reluctant First Lady*, reveals this understanding of her important friend. In volume 1 of *Eleanor Roosevelt*, Blanche Wiesen Cook wrote about their relationship in some depth, raising the possibility that it was lesbian. Then in 2016 Susan Quinn made Cook's conjectures more explicit in *Eleanor and Hick: The Love Affair That Shaped a First Lady*. Nevertheless, the only certainty is that Lorena and ER wrote letters that expressed physical longing (their correspondence, left to FDRL, was unsealed in 1978), that they were lifelong friends, and that the relationship changed over time. A selection of their letters is in Streitmatter, *Empty without You*.

3. MD oral history, CCOH.

4. Davis, *Invincible Summer*, 107–8.

5. Smith, *The Gatekeeper*, offers the best understanding of the relationship of FDR and Missy LeHand.

6. ER to Malvina Thompson, 17 August 1943, FDRL.

7. Quoted in Beasley, *Eleanor Roosevelt and the Media*, 137.

8. "Eleanor Roosevelt and Val-Kill: Emergence of a Political Leader," permanent exhibit, Eleanor Roosevelt National Historic Site, Hyde Park, N.Y.

9. Quoted in Lash, *Eleanor: The Years Alone*, 237.

Chapter Thirteen

1. An excellent source of information about "Eleanor's Little Village" is the Arthurdale Heritage, Inc. website, http://www.arthurdaleheritage.org/. Jeanne Goodman, executive director at Arthurdale, has been a helpful resource, meeting me for the annual New Deal Festival in the summer of 2016 at Arthurdale and later responding to my many questions. Most of the standard books about ER contain information about her interest in the New Deal resettlement project near Morgantown, West Virginia. Michael Golay, *America, 1933: The Great Depression, Lorena Hickok, Eleanor Roosevelt, and the Shaping of the New Deal* (New York: Free Press, 2013), an account of Lorena Hickok's journey across America to report to Harry Hopkins on the desperate conditions, provides background on Arthurdale.

2. Marilee Hall, "Arthurdale: First New Deal Planned Community," *Hudson River Valley Review* 26, no. 1 (2009): 50.

Chapter Fourteen

1. Geoffrey C. Ward estimates that FDR returned to Hyde Park at least two hundred times during his presidency, likely more often (*Before the Trumpet*, 348).

2. MD oral history, CCOH.

3. NC quoted in Cook, *Eleanor Roosevelt*, 2:532, from an undated letter from ER to NC, FDRL.

Chapter Fifteen

1. Quoted in Davis, *Invincible Summer*, 145.

2. Ibid.

3. MD oral history, CCOH. Quotations from MD in this chapter come from this oral history, unless noted otherwise.

4. Ibid.

5. Nina Roosevelt Gibson, e-mail to the author, November 8, 2014.

6. Nina Roosevelt Gibson, telephone interview with the author.

7. Malvina Thompson to Anna Roosevelt Boettiger, 11 July 1938, FDRL.

8. MD used the term "tragic talk" between NC and ER in her interviews with Kenneth S. Davis (*Invincible Summer*) and in the CCOH interviews. The most comprehensive discussion of the breakup of the friendship is in Cook, *Eleanor Roosevelt*, 2:530–37.

9. ER to Lorena Hickok, 19 January 1938, FDRL.

10. Quoted in Cook, *Eleanor Roosevelt*, 2:519–20.

11. ER to Lorena Hickok, 27 November 1933, FDRL.

Chapter Sixteen

1. Esther Lape, "Salt Meadow: From the Perspective of a Half Century," Lape Papers, FDRL.

2. Quoted in Cook, *Eleanor Roosevelt*, 2:532.

3. ER to Esther Lape, 5 October 1938, FDRL.

4. ER to MD and NC, 29 October 1938, MDP.

5. ER to MD, 9 November 1938, FDRL.

6. Quoted in Davis, *Invincible Summer*, 156.

7. Quoted in ibid., 155.

Chapter Seventeen

1. This chapter is based on the transcript of the oral history interviews with Frances Perkins (1951–55, CCOH). A digitized transcript of the long interview with Perkins, with an easy search tool for finding topics within the interview, is available at http://www.columbia.edu/cu/lweb/digital/collections/nny/perkinsf/.

2. Of special interest is Kirstin Downey's biography of Perkins, *The Woman behind the New Deal*.

3. Anna Rosenberg to MD, 31 August 1938, FDRL.

Chapter Eighteen

1. NC to ER, 8 February 1938, MDP.

2. In scattered undated letters from ER during this period there is some evidence that NC was receiving radiation treatments, but the reason is not clear.

3. Cook, *Eleanor Roosevelt*, 3:403–4.

4. Lash, *Eleanor and Franklin*, 643.

5. MD oral history, CCOH.

6. Davis, *Invincible Summer*, 166.

7. MD oral history, CCOH.

8. ER, "My Day," 27 December 1944, ERPP.

9. Quoted in Edna Gurewitsch, *Kindred Souls*, 79.

10. A fuller explanation for the cause of Eleanor Roosevelt's illness and death is given in ibid., 267–89.

Epilogue

1. MD oral history, CCOH.

2. Adlai Stevenson's memorial address is reprinted in various places, including at http://search.archives.jdc.org/multimedia/Documents/NY_AR55-64/NY55-64_ORG_058/NY55-64_ORG_058_1141.pdf (accessed 2016)

3. MD oral history, CCOH.

4. The story of ER's visits to Rock Creek Cemetery in Washington, D.C., to draw comfort from the Adams Memorial is included in most biographies. In my visits to Rock Creek Cemetery, I, as others, felt the power of the shrouded figure. A biography of Clover Adams is Dykstra, *Clover Adams*.

SELECTED BIBLIOGRAPHY

Archival Sources
Eleanor Roosevelt National Historic Site
Franklin D. Roosevelt Presidential Library and Museum, Hyde Park, N.Y.
  Marion Dickerman Papers
  Esther Lape Papers
  Anna Eleanor Roosevelt Papers
  Franklin D. Roosevelt Papers Pertaining to Family, Business, and
    Personal Affairs
  Roosevelt Family Papers, donated by the Children of Franklin D. and
    Eleanor Roosevelt
George Washington University, Washington, D.C.
  Eleanor Roosevelt Papers Project, https://www2.gwu.edu/~erpapers
    /documents/
Houghton Library, Harvard University, Cambridge, Mass.
  Anna Roosevelt Cowles Papers

Author's Interviews
Nina Roosevelt Gibson, e-mails, November 2014–November 2016
———, Salisbury, N.C., 10 February 2017
———, telephone interview, 10 November 2014
Edna Gurewitsch, telephone interview, 2014
Eleanor Roosevelt Seagraves, e-mails, November 2014–March 2017

Oral History Interviews
Columbia Center for Oral History, Butler Library, New York, N.Y.
  Marion Dickerman
  Frances Perkins
Eleanor Roosevelt Oral History Project, Franklin D. Roosevelt Library,
    Hyde Park, N.Y.
  Marion Dickerman
  Martha Gellhorn

Nina Roosevelt Gibson
Edna Gurewitsch
Reverend Gordon Kidd
Eleanor Roosevelt Seagraves
National Park Service, Roosevelt-Vanderbilt National Historic Sites,
    Hyde Park, N.Y.
Otto Berge
Charles Curnan

Books by Eleanor Roosevelt

The Autobiography of Eleanor Roosevelt. New York: Harper and Row, 1958, 1978; reprint, New York: Harper Perennial, 2014.

Hunting Big Game in the Eighties: The Letters of Elliott Roosevelt, Sportsman, Edited by His Daughter. New York: Charles Scribner's Son, 1933.

It's Up to the Women. New York: Frederick A. Stokes, 1933.

This I Remember. New York: Harper and Brothers, 1949.

This Is My Story. New York: Garden City Publishing, 1937.

Tomorrow Is Now. New York: Harper and Row, 1963.

You Learn by Living. New York: Harper and Brothers, 1960.

Other Sources

In addition to the sources listed here, there are excellent websites full of information of interest to readers of this book. They include an increasingly large number of digitized documents and photographs.

Asbell, Bernard, ed. *Mother and Daughter: The Letters of Eleanor and Anna Roosevelt*. New York: Coward, McCann, and Geoghegan, 1982.

Beasley, Maurine H. *Eleanor Roosevelt and the Media: A Public Quest for Self-Fulfillment*. Urbana: University of Illinois Press, 1987.

Beasley, Maurine H., Holly C. Shulman, and Henry R. Beasley. *The Eleanor Roosevelt Encyclopedia*. Westport, Conn.: Greenwood Press, 2001.

Bell-Scott, Patricia. *The Firebrand and the First Lady. Portrait of a Friendship: Pauli Murray, Eleanor Roosevelt, and the Struggle for Social Justice*. New York: Knopf, 2016.

Boettiger, John R. *A Love in Shadow: The Story of Anna Roosevelt and John Boettiger*. New York: Norton, 1978.

Cain, Richard R. *Eleanor Roosevelt's Val-Kill*. Charleston, S.C.: Arcadia, 2002.

Cook, Blanche Wiesen. *Eleanor Roosevelt.* 3 vols. New York: Viking Penguin, 1992–2016.

Davis, Kenneth S. *FDR: The Beckoning of Destiny, 1882–1928.* New York: G. P. Putnam's Sons, 1971.

———. *FDR: The New York Years, 1928–1933.* New York: Random House, 1985.

———. *FDR: The New Deal Years, 1933–1937.* New York: Random House: 1986.

———. *Invincible Summer: An Intimate Portrait of the Roosevelts Based on the Recollections of Marion Dickerman.* New York: Atheneum, 1974.

Downey, Kirstin. *The Woman behind the New Deal: The Life of Frances Perkins, FDR's Secretary of Labor and His Moral Conscience.* New York: Doubleday, 2009.

Dykstra, Natalie. *Clover Adams: A Gilded and Heartbreaking Life.* Boston: Houghton Mifflin Harcourt, 2012.

Faber, Doris. *The Life of Lorena Hickok: Eleanor Roosevelt's Friend.* New York: William Morrow, 1980.

Fredriksen, Beatrice. *Our Local Heritage: A Short History of the Town of Hyde Park.* Chicago: Hyde Park Historical Society, 1970.

Freidel, Frank. *Franklin D. Roosevelt: Launching the New Deal.* Vol. 3. Boston: Little, Brown, 1973.

Futral, Frank. "Val-Kill Industries: A History." *Hudson River Review* 26, no. 1 (Autumn 2009): 21–39.

Goodwin, Doris Kearns. *No Ordinary Time: Franklin and Eleanor Roosevelt: The Home Front in World War II.* New York: Simon and Schuster, 1994.

Gurewitsch, A. David. *Eleanor Roosevelt: Her Day.* New York: Interchange Foundation, 1973.

Gurewitsch, Edna P. *Kindred Souls: The Devoted Friendship of Eleanor Roosevelt and Dr. David Gurewitsch.* New York: Plume, 2003.

Hickok, Lorena. *Eleanor Roosevelt: Reluctant First Lady.* New York: Dodd, Mead, 1962.

Hoff-Wilson, Joan, and Marjorie Lightman, eds. *Without Precedent: The Life and Times of Eleanor Roosevelt.* Bloomington: Indiana University Press, 1984.

Kleeman, Rita Halle. *Gracious Lady: The Life of Sara Delano Roosevelt.* New York: D. Appleton-Century, 1935.

Klein, Jonas. *Beloved Island: Franklin and Eleanor and the Legacy of Campobello.* Forest Dale, Vt.: Paul S. Eriksson, 2000.

Knepper, Cathy D. *Dear Mrs. Roosevelt: Letters to Eleanor Roosevelt through Depression and War.* New York: Carroll and Graf, 2004.

Lash, Joseph P. *Eleanor and Franklin: The Story of Their Relationship, Based on Eleanor Roosevelt's Private Papers.* New York: Norton, 1971.

———. *Eleanor Roosevelt: A Friend's Memoir.* Garden City, N.Y.: Doubleday, 1964.

———. *Eleanor: The Years Alone.* New York: New American Library, 1972.

———. *Love, Eleanor: Eleanor Roosevelt and Her Friends.* Garden City, N.Y.: Doubleday, 1984.

MacLeish, Archibald. *The Eleanor Roosevelt Story.* Boston: Houghton Mifflin, 1965.

McClure, Ruth K., ed. *Eleanor Roosevelt, an Eager Spirit: The Letters of Dorothy Dow, 1933–45.* New York: Norton, 1984.

Miller, Kristie. *Isabella Greenway: An Enterprising Woman.* Tucson: University of Arizona Press, 2004.

Miller, Kristie, and Robert H. McGinnis, eds. *A Volume of Friendship: The Letters of Eleanor Roosevelt and Isabella Greenway, 1904–1953.* Tucson: Arizona Historical Society, 2009.

Moody, Kennon. *FDR and His Hudson Valley Neighbors.* Poughkeepsie, N.Y.: Hudson House, 2013.

Morris, Elisabeth Woodbridge. *Miss Wylie of Vassar.* New Haven, Conn.: Yale University Press, 1934.

Nesbitt, Henrietta. *White House Diary.* Garden City, N.Y.: Doubleday, 1948.

Nowlan, Alden. *Campobello: The Outer Island.* Toronto: Clarke, Irwin, 1995.

Pearson, Barbara E. *The Historic Structure Report on the Stone Cottage/Eleanor Roosevelt National Historic Site.* National Park Service, 1980.

Perkins, Frances. *The Roosevelt I Knew.* New York: Viking, 1946.

Quinn, Susan. *Eleanor and Hick: The Love Affair That Shaped a First Lady.* New York: Penguin, 2016.

Raz-Russo, Michal. *The Three Graces: Snapshots of Twentieth-Century Women.* New Haven, Conn.: Yale University Press, 2012.

Roosevelt, David B. *Grandmère: A Personal History of Eleanor Roosevelt.* With Manuela Dunn Mascetti. New York: Warner Books, 2002.

Roosevelt, Elliott, ed. *FDR: His Personal Letters, 1905–1928.* Vols. 1 and 2. New York, 1948.

Rowley, Hazel. *Franklin and Eleanor: An Extraordinary Marriage.* New York: Putnam, 2010.

Smith, Kathryn. *The Gatekeeper: Missy LeHand, FDR, and the Untold Story of the Partnership That Defined a Presidency.* New York: Simon and Schuster, 2016.

Steeholm, Clara, and Hardy Steeholm. *The House at Hyde Park.* New York: Viking, 1950.

Streitmatter, Rodger, ed. *Empty without You: The Intimate Letters of Eleanor Roosevelt and Lorena Hickok.* New York: DeCapo Press, 1998.

Suckley, Margaret L. "A Day at Hyde Park." *New Republic,* April 15, 1946, 527.

Tobin, James. *The Man He Became: How FDR Defied Polio to Win the Presidency.* New York: Simon and Schuster, 2013.

Tully, Grace. *FDR, My Boss.* New York: Scribner's, 1949.

Ward, Geoffey C. *Before the Trumpet: Young Franklin Roosevelt 1882–1905.* New York: Harper and Row, 2014.

———. "Eleanor Roosevelt Drew Her Strength from a Sanctuary Called Val-Kill." *Smithsonian* 15 (October 1984): 62–66, 68, 70–73.

———. *A First-Class Temperament: The Emergence of Franklin Roosevelt, 1905–1928.* New York: Vintage Books, 2014.

———, ed. *Closest Companion: The Unknown Story of the Intimate Friendship of Franklin Roosevelt and Margaret Suckley.* Boston: Houghton Mifflin, 1995.

Ward, Geoffrey C., and Ken Burns. *The Roosevelts: An Intimate History.* New York: Knopf, 2014.

Ware, Susan. *Letter to the World: Seven Women Who Shaped the American Century.* New York: Norton, 1998.

———. *Partner and I: Molly Dewson, Feminism, and New Deal Politics.* New Haven, Conn.: Yale University Press, 1987.

INDEX

Note: The abbreviation ER refers to Eleanor Roosevelt, MD refers to Marion Dickerman, NC refers to Nancy Cook, and FDR refers to Franklin Delano Roosevelt. Italic page numbers refer to illustrations.